Socialism and the Social Movement in the 19th Century

by Werner Sombart

PREFACE, BY THE TRANSLATOR

While rambling through quaint old Nuremberg, last summer, I was driven for shelter from rain into a bookshop. In a conversation with the genial proprietor, he called my attention to a book, lately published, that had already made a deep impression upon the world of German readers. A reading and re-reading of the little book convinced me that English readers, as well, will be glad to follow Professor Sombart in his comprehensive and suggestive review of Socialism.

Thanks are due to the learned German professor, whose name appears on the title-page, for his courtesy in this matter; also to his German publisher. I would also express obligation to my friend, Professor Sigmon M. Stern, with whom I have consulted freely on some difficult points of translation. The Introduction by Professor John B. Clark, of Columbia University, will be appreciated, I know, by the reader as well as by myself.

A.P.A.

APRIL, 1898.

INTRODUCTORY NOTE

The reader of this work will miss something which he has been accustomed to find in books on Socialism. Professor Sombart has not given us synopses of the theories of St. Simon, Proudhon, Marx, Owen, and others. His work marks the coming of a period in which socialism is to be studied, rather than the speculations of socialists. Theories and plans no longer constitute the movement. There are still schools of socialistic thought; but there is something actually taking place in the industrial world that is the important part of the socialistic movement. Reality is the essence of it.

The structure of the world of industry is changing. Great establishments are exterminating small ones, and are forming federations with each other.

Machinery is producing nearly every kind of goods, and there is no longer a place in the world for such a middle class as was represented by the master workman, with his slowly learned handicraft and his modest shop. These facts construed in a certain way are the material of socialism. If we see in them the dawn of an era of state industry that shall sweep competition and competitors out of the field, we are evolutionary socialists.

We may need a doctrinal basis for our view of the evolution that is going on; and we may find it in the works of Marx and others; but already we have ceased to have an absorbing interest in the contrasts and the resemblances that their several theories present. We have something to study that is more directly important than doctrinal history.

In Professor Sombart's study, Owenism, indeed, has an important place, since the striking element in it is something that the present movement has completely put away, namely, utopianism. No one now thinks, as did Owen, that merely perceiving the beauty of the socialistic ideal is enough to make men fashion society after that pattern. No one thinks that society can be arbitrarily shaped after any pattern. Marxism, in practice, means realism and a reliance on evolution, however little the wilder utterances of Marx himself may suggest that fact. Internationalism is also a trait of this modern movement; but it is not of the kind that is represented by the International Working-Men's Association. It is a natural affiliation of men of all nations having common ends to gain.

The relation of a thinker to a practical movement cannot lose its importance. It is this connection that Professor Sombart gives us, and his work is an early representative of the coming type of books on Socialism. It treats of realities, and of thought that connects itself with realities. It treats, indeed, of a purposeful movement to assist evolution, and to help to put the world into the shape that socialistic theorists have defined. Here lies the importance of the study of theory.

Professor Sombart's work contains little that is directly controversial; but it gives the impression that the purpose of the socialists is based on a fallacy, that it is not, in reality, in harmony with evolution, and that it will not prevail. It may be added that the style of the work is worthy of the thought that it expresses, and that the English translation is worthy of the original. The book will take its place among the more valuable of the works on Socialism that have thus far appeared.

JOHN B. CLARK, Columbia University, New York.

PREFACE

What is here published was originally delivered in the form of lectures, in the Fall of 1896, in Zurich, before miscellaneous but in general appreciative and inspiring audiences. The approval which they received, and the earnestly expressed wish of many hearers that the addresses might appear in print, have finally overcome a not inconsiderable reluctance on my part, felt by all in like position. The lectures are in many places enlarged; indeed, largely put into new form--changed from extemporaneous utterance into the more formal style proper for the written word. But their character remains, especially the restricted setting into which a great mass of material had to be compressed. This is done intentionally, since what I would offer to a larger public through this book is a brief, pointed, well-defined view of "Socialism and the Social Movement in the Nineteenth Century."

W.S.

CONTENTS

Class struggle--Kant--The meaning of the social movement--Essential elements in every social movement--Characterisation of the social movement--Conditions under which the working class lives--Russian peasants--Irish "rack-rent" tenants-- Uncertainty of existence--The Japanese--The Kurd-- Hegel--The ground of revolutionary passions in the modern proletariat--Time environment of the modern social movement--"Revolutionism."

Social literature, old and new--Adam Smith--David Ricardo--"Christian socialism"--Lamennais--Kingsley-- "Ethical socialism"--Sismondi--Carlyle--"Philanthropic socialism"--Pierre Leroux--Gruen--Hess-- Anti-capitalistic literature--Adam Mueller--Leopold von Haller--Capitalistic methods of production--Utopian socialists--St. Simon--Fourier--Owen.

Beginnings of the social movement carried on by the masses--Historic occurrences--Middle-class movements--French Revolution--Loi martiale--

"Coalition Law"--Marat--The men of Montaigne--The Sans-culottes--Danton--Robespierre--Constitution of 1793--Droits de l'Homme--Insurrection of Babeuf--The first proletarian agitation--Elizabethan trade law--The Chartist movement--English type of working-men's movement--French type--German type--Variations of the social movement--English social development--Carlyle's teaching.

Characterisation of the English working-men's movement--English industrial monopoly, 1850-1880-- Alternation of power between Tories and Whigs--Value of legislation in favour of the working man-- Temperament of the English working-man--Practical tendency of the old English trade-union--English "social peace"--French "revolutionism"--Factionism-- Clubbism--Putschism--Proudhon--The bourgeoisie-- Significance of the Reign of Terror--Difference between Roman type of the born revolutionist and the English working-man--Victor Hehn--French anarchism-- Bakunin--The peculiarities of social agitation in Germany--Ferdinand Lassalle--Schulze-Delitzsch--The Lassalle movement.

Birthplace, 1818--Parentage--Cosmopolitanism of the Marx family--At Bonn--Bruno Bauer--Driven from Prussia--From Paris--Finds rest in London--Death, 1883--Marxian theory of social agitation--Communistic Manifesto of Karl Marx and Frederic Engels--The theory of value--Marx's application of the evolution idea to the social movement--Ideal and material emancipation of the proletariat--Creation of class interest--Marxism as a social-political realism-- Engels's Struggle of Classes in France.

The proletarian-socialistic character of the revolution of 1848--Internationalism--First attempt for international combination--The

bounds--Must be carried on with proper weapons--English social agitation as a model.

APPENDIX. CHRONICLE OF THE SOCIAL MOVEMENT (1750-1896) 178

Notable inventions of modern machinery--"Machine Riots"--Petitions against machines and manufactories--Laws for the protection of machines--Adam Smith's "Wealth of Nations"--Robert Owen's chief writing's--Fourier's first great book--Complete removal of Elizabethan trade restrictions--The "Savannah" arrives at Liverpool--Chief work of St. Simon--More liberal coalition law--Opening of the Manchester-Liverpool Railroad--Insurrection of the silk workers in Lyons--Beginning of specific legislation for working men--Founding of the German Zollverein--Beginnings of German national industry--Introduction of Rowland Hill's penny postage--Telegraph first applied to English railroads--German governmental regulations for the repression of the working-men's movement--Severe laws of Napoleon III. for the repression of all social agitation--First World's Exposition in London--Bismarck forces the general, equal, secret, and direct ballot--Liberal trade regulation for the German Empire--Rapid development of capitalism in Germany, especially after the war--Trade-union act (English) supplemented in 1875--Law concerning the socialists in Germany--Beginning of governmental working-men's association in Germany--Insurance for the sick, against accident, for the sick and aged, in Germany--Endorsement of a legal establishment of the eight-hour work-day by the Trade-Union Congress in Liverpool--International Working-Men's Protection Conference in Berlin--Third International Working-Men's Congress in Zurich, at which English trade-unions deliberate officially with the Continental socialists--Fourth International Working-Men's Congress in London.

SOCIALISM AND THE SOCIAL MOVEMENT IN THE XIXTH CENTURY

CHAPTER I

WHENCE AND WHITHER

"Da ist's denn wieder, wie die Sterne wollten: Bedingung und Gesetz; und aller Wille Ist nur ein Wollen, weil wir eben sollten, Und vor dem Willen schweigt die Willkuer stille."

GOETHE, Urworte.

When Karl Marx began a communistic manifesto with the well-known words, "The history of all society thus far is the history of class strife," he uttered, in my opinion, one of the greatest truths that fill our century. But he did not speak the whole truth. For it is not fully true that all history of society consists exclusively in struggle between classes. If we would put "world history" into a single phrase we shall be obliged, I think, to say that there is an antithesis around which the whole history of society turns, as around two poles: social and national--using the word national in the widest meaning. Humanity develops itself into communities, and then these communities fight and compete with each other; but always within the community the individual begins to strive for elevation over others, in order, as Kant once expressed it, to make distinction of rank among his fellows, whom he does not like, from whom, however, he cannot escape. So we see on the one side the exertion of the community for wealth, power, recognition; and on the other side the same exertion, by the individual, after power, wealth, honour. These, as it seems to me, are the two matters which in fact fill all history. For history begins as this antithesis unfolds itself. It is merely a figure of speech, and you must not be shocked by the harsh expression, as I say that human history is a fight either for food division, or for feeding-place, upon our earth. These are both great contradictions which constantly emerge, which invariably control mankind. We stand to-day at the conclusion of an historic period of great national pride, and in the midst of a period of great social contrasts; and the varying views, world-wide in their differences, which obtain day by day in different groups of men, all lead back, as it seems to me, to the alternative, "national or social."

Before I now proceed with my theme, "Socialism and the Social Movement in the Nineteenth Century,"--that is, to one member of this antithesis, the social,--I would first suggest the question: "What is a social movement?" I answer: By a social movement we understand the aggregate of all those endeavours of a social class which are directed to a rational overturning of an existing social order to suit the interests of this class. The essential elements in every social movement are these: First, an existing order in which a certain society lives, and particularly a social order which rests chiefly upon the manner of production and distribution of material goods as the necessary basis of human existence. This specific system of production and distribution is the point of issue for every social movement. Secondly, a social class which is discontented with the existing conditions. By a "social class" I understand a number of similarly interested persons, especially persons who are similarly interested in economic matters--the distinctive point; that is, of men who are interested in a specific system of production and distribution. We must, in understanding any social class, go back to this economic system; and we should not allow ourselves to be blinded or confused by the inbred notions of certain classes. These prepossessions, which frequently control, are only bulwarks of classes differing economically. And, thirdly, an aim which this class, discontented with the existing order of things, holds up to reach; an ideal, which presents compactly all that for which the society will agitate, and which finds its expression in the postulates, demands, programmes of this class. In general, where you can speak of a social movement you find a point of issue, the existing social order; a supporter of the movement, the social class; an aim, the ideal of the new society.

In what follows I shall attempt to give some points of view for an understanding of a specific--the modern--social movement. But what do we mean by the phrase "to understand a social movement"? This: to comprehend the social movement in its essential historic limitations, in its causal connection with historic facts out of which, of necessity, that is produced which we describe as a social movement. That is, to comprehend why specific social classes are formed, why they present these particular points of opposition, why especially a pushing, aggressive social class has, and must have, that particular ideal for which it reaches. We mean, above all, to see that the movement springs not out of the whim, the choice, the malevolence of individuals; that it is not made, but becomes.

And now to the modern social movement. How is it to be characterised? If we would hold fast to those elements which constitute every social movement, we must describe the modern social movement on two sides: according to its aim, and according to the class that supports the movement. The modern social movement is, from the standpoint of its aim, a socialistic agitation, because, as will be shown, it is uniformly directed to the establishment of communal ownership, at least of the means of production; that is, to a socialistic, communal order of society in place of the existing method of private ownership. It is characterised, on the other side, in accordance with the adherents of the movement, by the fact that it is a proletarian agitation, or, as we customarily say, it is a working-men's movement. The class which supports it, upon which it rests, which gives to it the initiative, is the proletariat, a class of free wage-workers.

And now we ask the question: Is it possible to distinguish those circumstances which would make such a movement evidently a necessary historic development? I said that the social movement has, as its supporters, the modern proletariat, a class of free, lifelong wage-workers. The first condition of its existence is the rise of this class itself. Every social class is the result, the expression, of some specific form of production; the proletariat, of that form of production which we are accustomed to call capitalistic. The history of the rise of the proletariat is also the history of capitalism. This latter cannot exist, it cannot develop, without producing the proletariat. It is not now my purpose to give to you a history of capitalism. Only this much may be presented for the understanding of its nature: the capitalistic system of production involves the co-operation of two socially separated classes in the manufacture of material goods. One class is that which is in possession of the matter and means of production, as machines, tools, establishments, raw material, etc.--the capitalistic class; the other class is that of the personal factors of production, the possessors only of workman's craft--the free wage-workers. If we realise that all production rests upon the union of the material and the personal factors of production, then the capitalistic system of production distinguishes itself from others in that both the factors of production are represented through two socially separated classes which must necessarily come together by free consent, the "free wage compact," so that the processes of production may take place. The method of production thus formed has entered into history as a necessity. It arose in that moment when demand had become so strong that the earlier methods of production could not longer satisfy the enlarging conditions, in the time when new and large markets were opened. It appeared originally solely with the historic task of implanting the mercantile spirit of manufacture for the maintaining of these new markets. The mercantile talent forces itself on as leader of production and draws great masses of mere hand-workers into its service. It then becomes yet more of a necessity as the development of the technique of production complicates the whole operation so greatly that the combination of many kinds of work in one product is unavoidable; especially since the introduction of steam for the production and transportation of goods. The supporters of the capitalistic method of production are, as a class, the bourgeoisie, the middle class. How gladly would I speak of the great historic mission which this class has fulfilled! But again I must content myself with this mere reference, that we see this historic mission in the wonderful development which this class has given to the material forces of production. Under the compulsion of competition, lashed by the passion of accumulation which enters with it into modern history, this class has wrought into reality for us those fairy tales of the Thousand and One Nights, those wonders in which daily we rejoice, as through the streets or the industrial expositions of our great cities we stroll, as we talk with the antipodes, as we sail in floating palaces over the ocean, or bask in the glory of our luxurious parlours. But our point is this: the existence of this capitalistic system of production is the necessary condition for that class which is the supporter of the modern socialistic movement--the proletariat. I have already said that the proletariat follows the capitalistic form of production as its shadow. This scheme of production cannot exist otherwise, cannot develop itself otherwise, than under the condition that, subject to the command of individuals, troops of possessionless workers are herded in great undertakings. It has as a necessary presupposition the rending of all society into two classes: the owners of the means of production, and the personal factors in production. Thus the existence of capitalism is the necessary preliminary condition of the proletariat, and so of the modern social movement.

But how stands it with the proletariat? What are the conditions under which the working-class lives? And how has it come to pass that out of these conditions those particular tendencies and demands have arisen which, as we shall find, have come out of this proletariat? Usually, when one is asked concerning the characteristics of the modern proletariat, the first answer is-- the great misery in which the masses are sunk. That may pass with some qualification; only it must not be forgotten that misery is not specifically confined to the modern proletariat. Thus, how miserable is the condition of the peasants in Russia, of the Irish "rack-rent" tenants! There must be a specific kind of misery which characterises the proletariat. I refer, here, particularly to those unhealthy work-places, mines, manufactories with their noise and dust and heat, that have arisen with the modern method of production; I think of the conditions produced by these methods of production which tend to draw into the work certain categories of workers,-- as women and children; I think further of how the concentration of population in industrial centres and in the great cities has increased the misery of external life for the individual. At all events, we may consider the intensification of misery as a primary cause for the growth and insistence of new thoughts and new feelings. But that is not the most important point, when we ask after the essential conditions of existence of the proletariat. It is much more characteristic that in the moment when great masses sink into misery, upon the other side, shining like a fairy's creation, the millionaire arises. It is the contrast between the comfortable villa and elegant equipage of the rich, the magnificent stores, the luxurious restaurants which the workman passes as he goes on his way to his manufactory or workshop in the dreary part of the city; it is the contrast in condition which develops hate in the masses. And that, again, is a peculiarity of the modern system, that it develops this hate and permits hate to become envy. It seems to me that this happens principally for the reason that those who display this grandeur are no longer the churches or the princes; but that they are those very persons on whom the masses feel themselves dependent, in whose direct economic control they see themselves, in whom they recognise their so-called "exploiters." This definite modern contrast is that which principally excites the intensity of this feeling of hate in the masses. Yet one thing further. It is not merely the miserable condition, the contrast with the well-to-do; but another terrible whip is swung over the heads of the proletariat--I mean the uncertainty in their lives. Also in this we have to do with a peculiarity of modern social life, if we rightly understand it. Uncertainty of existence is indeed elsewhere: the Japanese trembles at the thought of the earthquake that may at any moment overwhelm him and his possessions; the Kurd is afraid of the sand-storm in summer, of the snow-storm in winter, which blight the feeding-place for his flocks; a flood or drought in Russia may rob the peasant of his harvest and expose him to starvation. But what constitutes the specific uncertainty of the proletariat, which expresses itself in the loss of wage and work, is this, that this uncertainty is understood as a result not of the natural causes of which I have spoken, but of the specific form of organisation of economic life--that is the chief point. "Against nature no man can assert a right; but in the constitution of society lack becomes immediately a form of injustice done to one or another class"--(Hegel). Further, this uncertainty as to matters of nature leads to superstition or bigotry; but this social uncertainty, if I may so express it, develops a sharpening and refinement of judgment. Man seeks after the causes which lead to this uncertainty. It works simply an increase of that feeling of resistance which grows up in the masses; it permits hate and envy to rise threateningly. Here, then, is the ground on which the revolutionary passions, hate, envy, insubordination, grow in the modern proletariat: peculiar forms of misery, the contrast of this wretchedness with the glitter of the bread-masters, the uncertainty of existence, supposed to arise out of the forms of organisation of economic life.

In order now to be able to understand how these growths have pressed forward into the peculiar manifestations which characterise the modern social movement, we must realise that the masses which we have learned to know in the position thus described have been developed as if by magic, have not slowly grown into this condition. It is as if earlier history had been completely effaced for millions of men. For, as the presupposition of capitalism is combination in large operations, there is involved in this also the accumulation of masses of men in cities and centres of industry. This massing, however, means nothing other than this, that completely incoherent, amorphous crowds of men out of the most widely separated regions of the land are thrown together at one point, and that upon them the demand is made "Live!" This involves a complete break with the past, a tearing apart of all ties of home, village, family, custom. It means as well the overthrow of all the earlier ideals of these homeless, possessionless, and coherentless masses. This is a matter which is often underestimated. We forget that it is an entirely new life which the hordes of the modern proletariat have to begin. But what kind of a life is it? In its characteristics I find as many points of explanation for the positive construction of the proletarian world of ideas as for the destruction of all that has heretofore been dear and precious to man. I mean, the socialistic ideals of communal life and work must of necessity spring out of the industrial centres and the resorts of the working-men in the great cities. In the tenement-houses, the huge manufactories, the public houses for meetings and for pleasures, the individual proletarian, as if forsaken by God and man, finds himself with his companions in misery again together, as members of a new and gigantic organism. Here are new societies forming, and these new communities bear the communistic stamp, because of modern methods of work. And they develop, grow, establish themselves in the mass of men, in proportion as the charm of separate existence fades from the individual; the more dreary the attic room in the suburb of the city, the more attractive is the new social centre in which the outcast finds himself again treated as a man. The individual disappears, the companion emerges. A uniform class consciousness matures itself, also the habit of communal work and pleasure. So much for the psychology of the proletariat.

In order now to gain a full understanding of the modern social movement, let us look at its general time environment. Also here merely a remark or two must suffice. Perhaps this phrase will sufficiently describe the modern period: there is in it conspicuously an exuberance of life, as I think in no earlier period. A stream of vigorous life flows through modern society as at no earlier time; and for this reason a quickness of contact between all the individual members of a society is made possible now as never heretofore. This has been accomplished by the modern means of transportation which capitalism has created for us. The possibility in these days of informing oneself in a few hours concerning the occurrences throughout a great country by means of telegraph, telephone, newspaper, and the possibility of throwing great masses of men from one place to another by modern means of transportation, have produced a condition of solidarity throughout great groups of men, a sense of omnipresence, which was unknown in all earlier times. Particularly is this true in the large cities of these days. The ease of movement of masses has grown enormously. And in like manner has that grown which we are accustomed to call education--knowledge, and with knowledge demands.

With this vigour of life, however, is most closely united that which I would call the nervosity of modern times, an unsteadiness, haste, insecurity of existence. Because of the distinctive character of economic relations, this trace of unrest and haste has forced itself into all branches not only of economic but as well of social life. The age of free competition has stamped itself upon all spheres of life. Every man strives with others, no one feels himself sure, no one is contented with his condition. The beauty and calm of rest are gone.

One thing more. I will call it "revolutionism," and I mean by that term the fact that never has there been another time, like ours, of such entire change in all the conditions of life. All is in flux--economics, science, art, morals, religion. All ideas on these matters are in such a process of change that we are impelled to the delusion that there is nothing now certain. And this is perhaps one of the most important considerations for the explanation of the real meaning of modern social agitation. It explains in two ways. In it we see the reason for that destructive criticism of all that exists, which allows nothing as good, which throws away all earlier faith as old iron in order to enter with new material upon the market. Also, it explains the fanatical belief in the feasibility of the desired future state. Since so much has already changed, since such wonders, for which no one has dared to hope, have been realised before our very eyes, why not more? Why not all that man wishes? Thus the revolutionism of the present becomes fertile soil for the Utopia of the future. Edison and Siemens are the spiritual fathers of Bellamy and Bebel.

These seem to me the essential conditions under which a social movement has developed itself in this later time: the peculiar existence of the proletariat; the specific misery, contrast, uncertainty, springing from the modern economic system; a reorganisation of all forms of life, through the tearing apart of earlier relations and the upbuilding of entirely new social forms upon a communistic basis, and of new consolidations in the great cities and operations; finally, the peculiar spirit of the time in which the social movement exhibits itself, intensity of life, nervosity, revolutionism.

Now let us consider this social movement itself, in theory and practice.

CHAPTER II

CONCERNING UTOPIAN SOCIALISM

"Rarely do we reach truth except through extremes--we must have foolishness ... even to exhaustion, before we arrive at the beautiful goal of calm wisdom."

SCHILLER, Philosophical Letters, Preamble.

It would be strange if such a mighty revolution in economic and social matters as I have sketched for you should not have found its reflection in the minds of thinking men. It would be wonderful, I think, if with this overturning of social institutions a revolution of social thought, science, and faith should not follow. We find in fact that parallel with this revolution in life fundamental changes have taken place in the sphere of social thought. By the side of the old social literature a new set of writings arises. The former belongs to the end of the previous and the beginning of the present century; it is that which we are accustomed to call the classic political economy; it is that which, after a development of about one hundred and fifty to two hundred years, found the highest theoretical expression of the capitalistic economic system through the great political economists Adam Smith and David Ricardo. By the side of this literature, devoted to the capitalistic view of economics, now grows a new school of writings which has this general characteristic, that it is anti-capitalistic; that is, it places itself in conscious opposition to the capitalistic school of economics and considers the advocacy of this opposition as its peculiar task.

In accordance with the undeveloped condition of such economic thought it is, of course, a medley of explanations and claims as to what is and what should be, wherein the new literature expresses its opposition. All undeveloped literature begins in this tumultuous way, just as all unschooled minds at first slowly learn to distinguish between what is and what should be. And indeed in the immaturity of this new literature the practical element predominates greatly, as may readily be understood; there is a desire to justify theoretically the agitation, the new postulates, the new ideals.

For this reason, if we would see this literature in its full relations and distinguish its various nuances (delicate differences), it will be convenient to choose as distinguishing marks the differing uses of the new "Thou shalt." Thus we recognise in general two groups in this new literature, the reformatory and the revolutionary. The latter word is not used in its ordinary meaning, but in that which I shall immediately define. The reformatory and the revolutionary literature divide on this point, that the reformatory recognises in principle the existing economic system of capitalism, and attempts upon the basis of this economy to introduce changes and improvements, which are, however, subordinate, incidental, not essential; also and especially, that the fundamental features of social order are retained, but that man desires to see his fellow-man changed in thought and feeling. A new spirit obtains, repentance is proclaimed, the good qualities of human nature win the upper hand--brotherly love, charity, conciliation.

This reformatory agitation that recognises the injury and evil of social life, but that with essential adhesion to the dominant economic system desires to mitigate the injury and to overcome or minimise the evil, has different ways of expression. It is a Christian, or an ethical, or a philanthropic impulse which calls forth the new literature and controls the writings that make for social reform.

The Christian thought is that which, in application to the social world, creates that trend of literature which we are accustomed incorrectly to designate under the phrase "Christian socialism." Of this are the writings of Lamennais in France, Kingsley in England, which, filled with the spirit of the Bible, address to employer and employe alike the demand--Out with the spirit of mammon from your souls, fill your hearts with the spirit of the gospel, the "new spirit," as they constantly call it. And quite similarly sound the voices of those earlier "ethical" economists, Sismondi, Thomas Carlyle, who do not become tired of preaching, if not the "Christian," at least the "social" spirit. Change of heart is their watchword. The third drift of thought, which I call the philanthropic, directs itself rather towards the emotions than towards the sense of duty or the religious element in man. Pierre Leroux in France, Gruen and Hess in Germany, are men who, filled with a great, overpowering love for mankind, desire to heal the wounds which their sympathetic hearts behold, who would overwhelm the misery which they see by this universal love of man. "Love one another as men, as brothers!" is the theme of their preaching. All these three streams of thought, merely the sources of which I have specified, continue influential to the present day; and all of them have this in common, that they hold fast in principle to the foundations of the existing social order--therefore I call them reformatory. Opposed to them appears another class of literature, the "revolutionary"; so called because its great principle is the doing away with the foundations of capitalistic economy, and the substituting something different. This it proposes to do in two different ways,--if I may express my meaning in two words,--backwards and forwards.

At the very time when economic contradictions develop themselves and new phases of anti-capitalistic literature come to the surface, we find a revolutionary anti-capitalistic literature strongly asserting itself, which demands a retrogression from the existing system of economics. Such are the writings of Adam Mueller and Leopold von Haller in the first third of our century, men who would change the bases on which the modern capitalistic economy is founded by introducing the crumbled feudalistic guild system of the middle ages in place of the middle-class capitalistic system of to-day. These are indeed manifestations which have not as yet reached their end.

Besides these reactionary manifestations, there is another movement which does not want this regression to old forms, but in the same way demands an overthrow of the principles of the existing capitalistic system. But this change must be under the influence of those modern advanced ideas which, especially on the technical side, betoken that which we are accustomed to call "progress." Systems, that is, theories, they are which hold fast to an historic essence of capitalistic methods of production--that it is built upon the basis of modern production in the mass; but which, under the influence of advanced ideas, call for a new order of production and distribution in the interests of those classes of the people which under the capitalistic economy seem to come short--thus essentially in the interests of the great masses of the proletariat. The theorists who desire such a development of the capitalistic economy in the interests of the proletariat, while upholding methods of production on a large scale, are the ones whom we must call socialists in the true meaning of the word. And we have now to do with a strange species of these socialists, with those whom we are accustomed to call utopists or utopian socialists. The typical representatives of these utopian socialists are St. Simon and Charles Fourier in France, and Robert Owen in England. Of these, the most conspicuous are the two Frenchmen; their systems are most frequently presented. Owen is less known. As I now attempt to make clear to you, through him, the essence of utopian socialism, it is because he is less known, but especially because in my opinion he is the most interesting of the three great utopists. It is he who on the one side most clearly shows to us the genesis of the modern proletarian ideal, and on the other side has been of greatest influence upon other socialistic theorists, especially upon Karl Marx and Friedrich Engels.

Robert Owen was a manufacturer. We find him at the age of twenty years already the manager of a great cotton-mill. Soon after he established a mill at Lanark. Here he learned practical life by personal experience. We distinguish two periods in his life. In the first he is what we may call an educationalist, a man who interests himself especially in the education of youth and expects through it an essential reformation of human society. The chief work of this epoch is the book A New View of Society. In the second period he is a socialist; and his most important work is A Book of the New Moral World. Owen really interests us in this second period, as a socialist. What does he thus teach? And what is the essence of this first form of utopian socialism?

Robert Owen takes as the starting-point for his theorising the investigations which he made in his immediate surroundings. He pictures to us the state of affairs in connection with his own manufactories; how the workers, especially the women and children, degenerated, physically, intellectually and morally. He begins also with a recognition of the evils which distinguish the modern capitalistic system; his starting-point is proletarian. Upon these investigations of his own he now builds a social-philosophic system which is not unknown to one who has studied the social philosophy of the eighteenth century. Owen's social philosophy is essentially characterised by this, that he believes in man as good by nature, and in an order of communal life which would in like manner be naturally good if only these men were brought into proper relations with each other--faith in the so-called ordre naturel, in a natural order of things which has possibly existed somewhere, but which in any case would exist, were it not that artificial hindrances stand in the way, evils which make it impossible for man to live in this natural way with others. These evils, these forces, which stand in the way of the accomplishment of a natural communal life, Robert Owen sees of two kinds: one in the faulty education of men, the other in the defective environment in which modern man lives--the evils of a rich milieu. He infers logically, if we would again realise that natural and beautiful condition of harmonious communal life, that ordre naturel, both these evils must be driven out of the world. He demands, therefore, better education on the one side, a better environment upon the other. In these two postulates we find side by side the two periods of his development as we have heretofore seen them. In the first he lays stress rather upon education; in the second, rather upon change of environment. He recognises, further--and this is perhaps the particular service rendered by Owen to socialistic theory--that these evil conditions, on the overcoming of which all depends, have not been provided by nature, but have grown out of a definite system of social order, which he believes to be the capitalistic. In the capitalistic economy he sees nothing of that natural law which the representatives of the classical economies assert; but an order of society created by man. Even his opponents believed in the ordre naturel, only they thought that it was realised; Owen did not. Much more, Owen was compelled to demand the overthrow of this economic system in order that his goal might be reached, that man might be able to enjoy a better development and a better environment. For this reason he demanded that the artificial economic system should undergo essential changes, especially in two points, the main pillars upon which the economic system is built. Owen repudiated the competition of the individual and the profit-making of the master.

If this be allowed, the further practical arrangements which Owen demanded must in like manner be granted: in place of individualism, socialism must stand. In this way private operation will be replaced by communal production, and competition will be in fact overthrown; also, the profit of the employer will flow into the pockets of the producers, the members of the social organisation. These ideas of socialistic production grew, for Owen, spontaneously out of the capitalistic system in which he lived.

Here we come directly to the attitude of spirit in which Robert Owen has conceived his socialistic system, and it is necessary for the completion of this sketch to make reference especially to the means which Owen would use to reach his goal. These means are essentially a universal understanding and agreement among men; to them the truth and beauty of this new order should be preached, so that the wish may be aroused in them to accomplish this new order. But Owen does not think of the possibility that, when it is once made clear how wonderful this new order would be and how wonderfully men would live therein, men would not wish for the new order, and even if they did wish for it, that they might not be able to accomplish it. Only let the matter be known, then the wish and the ability will follow. For this reason, it is possible that the new order may enter at any moment; "as a thief in the night," Owen expresses it, socialism can come over the world. Only intellectual perception is necessary, and this can illumine the mind of man suddenly as a lightning flash. This peculiar conception of the means and ways that lead to the goal is one of the characteristic traits which distinguish the system of Owen, and in like manner of all utopian socialists.

If we look at this system as a whole, we find as the starting-point a criticism of existing social circumstances in a proletarian community. We find, further, as the basis upon which the system stands, the social philosophy of the eighteenth century. We see, as its demands, the overthrow of the capitalistic economy and the replacing of private production by communal operation. We find, finally, as the means for accomplishing this, as the roadway that leads to the object desired, the enlightenment of mankind. How he then exerted himself to carry out his plans in detail, how he created a New Lanark, and how his plans were entirely frustrated--all that interests us now as little as does the fact that Owen reached large practical results, in the shortening of the hours of labor and in the limitation of work by women and children, through improvement and amelioration of work in his manufactories, in which a new race began to rise in intellectual and moral freshness. Just so little are we interested in the fact that he is the father of English trade-union agitation. We would only look at his significance for the social movement, and this lies especially in the fact that he first, at least in outline, created that which since has become the proletarian ideal. For this point must be made clear to us, that all the germs of later socialism are contained in Owen's system.

If I now, after having sketched the fundamental ideas of Owen's system, may attempt to condense the essence of the so-called utopian socialism into a few sentences, I would specify this as essential: Owen and the others are primarily socialists because their starting-point is proletarian criticism. They draw this immediately out of spheres in which capitalism asserts itself, out of the manufactory as Owen, out of the counting-house as Fourier. They are, further, socialists for this reason, not only that their starting-point is proletarian, but also because their object is socialistic in the sense that it would put joint enterprise in the place of private operation; that is, a new economic order which does not longer provide for private operation and the sharing of the profit between master and workman, but is based upon communal effort, without competition and without employer. But why, we ask ourselves, are they called socialistic utopists? And how are they to be distinguished from those theorists whom we shall learn to call scientific socialists? Owen, St. Simon, and Fourier are to be called utopists for the reason that they do not recognise the real factors of socialism; they are the true and legitimate children of the naive and idealistic eighteenth century, which we, with right, call the century of intellectual enlightenment.

I have already showed to you how this belief in enlightenment, in the power of the knowledge of good, predominates in Owen's system. In this lies essentially its utopianism, because those are looked upon as effective and impelling factors which do not in fact constitute social life and the real world. Thus this belief mistakes doubly: it contains a false judgment of present and past, and it deceives itself concerning the prospects of the future. So far as his followers assume that the present order of things is nothing other than a mistake, that only for this reason men find themselves in their present position, that misery rules in the world only because man has not known thus far how to make it better--that is false. The utopists fail to see, in their optimism, that a part of this society looks upon the status quo as thoroughly satisfactory and desires no change, that this part also has an interest in sustaining it, and that a specific condition of society always obtains because those persons who are interested in it have the power to sustain it. All social order is nothing other than the temporary expression of a balance of power between the various classes of society. Now judge for yourselves what mistaken estimate of the true world, what boundless underestimate of opposing forces, lie in the belief that those who have power can be moved to a surrender of their position through preaching and promise.

As the utopists underestimate the power of their opponents, so they overestimate their own strength, and thus become utopists as to the future. They are pervaded by the strong conviction that there is needed only an energetic, hearty resolution in order to bring to reality the kingdom of the future. They rate too highly the ability of the men who will constitute the future society. They forget, or they do not know, that in a long process of reconstruction men and things must first be created in order to make the new social order possible.

For the practical working of the social movement, the most interesting conclusion which the utopists draw logically out of this conception is the kind of tactics which they recommend for reaching the new condition. From what has been said it follows necessarily that this strategy must culminate in an appeal to men collectively. It will not be accomplished by a specific and interested class; but it expects from all men that, when the matter is rightly explained, they will wish for the good. Indeed, it is assumed that it is only ignorance on the part of the opponent that keeps him from accepting openly and freely this good, from divesting himself of his possessions and exchanging the old order for the new. The characteristic example of this childish way of viewing things is the well-known fact that Charles Fourier daily waited at his home, between the hours of twelve and one, to receive the millionaire who should bring to him money for the erection of the first phalanstery. No one came.

In closest connection with this belief in the willingness of the ruling classes to make concessions stands the disinclination to all use of force, to all demand and command. Thus we find, as the simple thought in the tactics of the utopists, the repudiation of class strife and political effort. For how can this be brought into harmony with their main idea? How can anything that is to be accomplished by intellectual illumination, or at most by example, be achieved through strife? It is unthinkable. So, just as utopian socialism rejects political exertion, it also stands opposed to all those efforts which we are accustomed to call the economic agitation of the workman, such as trade-unions and the like. It is the same thought: how shall the organisation of working-men for strife tend to the improvement of the condition of work, when this can come only through the preaching of the new gospel? Robert Owen indeed organised in England trade-unions. But their work was really the propagation of his socialistic theories, not painful struggle against capitalism. Rejection of class strife in the sphere of politics as of economic agitation, repudiation of this in speech and writing and example--herein culminate the tactics of the utopian socialists. This, as I have attempted to show to you, is the necessary outcome of their system, built upon beautiful but narrow lines.

As we now take leave of utopian socialism we must guard ourselves from the thought that the spirit of this great historic influence has fully disappeared from the world. No! no day passes without the reappearance, in some book or speech, of these fundamental thoughts which we have recognised as the essence of utopian socialism. Especially in the circles of the well inclined middle-class social politicians does this spirit live to-day; but even in the proletariat itself it is not by any means dead. We shall see how it is revived later, in connection with revolutionary thought. For this reason a more than merely historic interest invests this particular line of thought.

CHAPTER III

THE ANTECEDENTS OF THE SOCIAL MOVEMENT

"The great, dumb, deep-buried class lies like an Enceladus, who in his pain, if he will complain of it, has to produce earthquakes."--THOMAS CARLYLE,

"Chartism," ix. (Essays. Edition, Chapman and Hall, vi., 169).

The question which now rests upon the lips of you all, since I have indicated the lines of thought of the first socialists, is this: When such noble minds drew the plan of a new and better world for their suffering brethren, where was the proletariat itself, and what did it do? What are the beginnings of the social movement which is carried on by the masses?

The answer must be that long, very long, after much had been thought and written concerning the condition and future of the proletariat this element of the population yet remained completely untouched by these new ideas, knew nothing of them, cared nothing for them; it permitted itself to be controlled by other forces, other motives. The systems of St. Simon, Fourier, Owen, have had little or no influence with the masses.

As we turn to the proletariat itself and ask after its fate,--perhaps up to the middle of our century,--we find a precursor of the social movement which everywhere--that is, in all lands controlled by the capitalistic economy-- exhibits the same marks and is uniformly characterised in the following way: where the movement of the masses stands out clearly and conscious of its aim, it is not proletarian; where it is proletarian, it is not clear and conscious of its aim. That means, in the conscious movement in which the proletariat is found engaged, middle-class elements direct as to the object sought: where the proletariat undertakes to be independent, it shows all the immaturity of the formative stages of a social class, mere instincts, no clearly defined postulates and aims.

Those historic occurrences in which the proletariat played a role, although they were not proletarian movements, are the well-known revolutions which we connect with the years 1789, 1793, 1830, 1832, 1848--for I must go back into the previous century for the inner connection. We have here movements which are essentially middle-class; in them political liberties are sought, and, so far as the proletarian elements are concerned, the masses fight the battles of the middle classes, like the common soldiers who fought in feudal armies.

This fact, that we here have to do with purely middle-class movements, has so often been mistaken by many celebrated historians, the terms "communism" and "socialism" have been so constantly applied to those agitations, that it is well worth our while to show the incorrectness of this assumption. For this purpose, we must look separately at those movements which are connected with the years thus specified, since each one has its own characteristics.

If we present to ourselves first the real meaning of the movements of 1789 and 1793, the great French Revolution, it is clear even to those of limited vision that the revolution of 1789 was purely a middle-class movement, and indeed carried on by the higher part of the middle-class. It is the struggle of the upper middle-class for the recognition of its rights, and for relief from the privileges of the ruling class of society--from the fetters in which it had been held by feudal powers. It expresses this struggle in demands for equality and freedom, but it really means from the very start a limited equality and freedom. Look at the first, trenchant, we may call them social, laws which were passed by the new regime of France. They are by no means of a popular character, or partial to the working-man; we see at the first look that they were not made by the masses for the masses, but by an aristocratic middle-class, which places itself in sharp opposition to the rabble. Thus the well-known Loi martiale of October 20, 1789, a riot act, gives expression to this distinction as it speaks of the "bons citoyens" who must be protected by stern police regulation against the attacks of the gens mal intentiones; "when the mob does not disperse on warning, then the armed forces shall fire." They would so control the caprices of the masses that not a second time should a dagger find its way into the breast of an honourable baker, when the populace without authority would appropriate to itself the bread in the bakeries.

I think of a second important law, born out of the doctrinaire middle-class spirit of these first years; the "Coalitions Law" of June 17, 1791. It punishes every combination of tradesworkers for the furtherance of their "alleged" common interests, as an attempt upon the freedom and rights of man, by a fine of five hundred livres and the loss of citizenship for a year. This applies equally to the employer and the working-man, we may better say the master and the journeyman; but we all know what crying injustice this equality has produced.

Then comes the first consolidation of the new society, the Constitution of November 3, 1791, which, through the introduction, of limited franchise, brings to sharp and clear expression the separation between a ruling class of those well-to-do and a ruled class of the "have-nothings." There are now "full citizens" and citizens of the second class.

Thus it is clear that the revolution of 1789 was not at all a proletarian movement. There may seem to be some doubt concerning the agitation of 1793, for it is this, before all others, which our great historians, as Sybel, like to specify as "communistic." The men of Montaigne are, in their eyes, the predecessors of the social democracy; and, indeed, quite lately in a small book published by the Berlin Professor H. Delbrueck in the Goettingen library for working-men, exactly this assertion is presented--that the leaders of this social movement were true social democrats, and that in fact the social democracy has developed no new thoughts since Saint Just and Robespierre. I cannot recognise this assertion as correct. Let us test it.

I assert that even the movement of 1793 was essentially non-proletarian. We grant that in it an undercurrent of democracy breaks forth, which the French Revolution always had; and it is this which has misled many. This was there from the beginning. It expressed itself already in 1789, in the elections to the States-General, and comes finally in 1793 to its full development.

As you read through the Cahiers with their Doleances of the year 1789, those "papers of grievances" which the electors, especially those of Paris and Lyons, were accustomed to hand to their representatives, you find therein already a peculiar tone which does not harmonise with the honeyed expressions of the men of the "tennis court." These demands were connected with the ruling hard times, for the winter of 1789 had been severe; and they complained because misery could not be lessened by a free constitution. "The voice of freedom means nothing to the heart of a miserable man who is dying of hunger." Already they demanded bread taxes and employment, the overthrow of Sunday rest and of feast-days. Everyone knows how this cry arises again and again in the speeches and writings of Marat. The Ami du Peuple declaims against the "aristocrats," and desires to serve the "people." They found out that, for the great masses of the "poor," freedom and equality availed nothing; and Marat thus concludes: "Equality of rights leads to equality of enjoyment, and only upon this basis can the idea rest quietly." Then come the taxes; the "maximum" comes. But I ask you, does that make this movement a proletarian and social one? Can it be that at all? Let us look merely at its supporters! The chief centres of democratic undercurrent are, as has been said, Lyons and Paris. In Lyons we find, indeed, a proletariat, that of the silk industry. We have the statistics of the year 1789; at that time there were, in the Lyons silk industry, 410 maitres marchands fabricants, 4402 maitres ouvriers, 1796 compagnons, and about 40,000 other workers of both sexes. We must allow that here, without doubt, there are indeed strong proletarian interests and instincts; yet they are veiled by the peculiar character of the Lyons silk industry. It had at that time, and has even to-day, a strong hold upon the lower middle-class, and to a degree upon the upper middle-class, for two reasons. One, due to its peculiar organisation, the fact that this work was not carried on in large manufactories but in small workshops under the direction of independent masters, and that this created a class of independent men, between the capitalist and the worker, hard to move to concerted action with the proletariat. A second reason is this, that the Lyons silk industry is a manufacture of an article of luxury. Such industries are in their very nature, even in the earlier times, anti-revolutionary; the men of Montaigne would not use silk stockings. For this reason we find Lyons, naturally, after the first enthusiasm is over, by the side of the Vendee at the head of the counter-revolution, even at the beginning of the year 1790. In general, as Lyons becomes anti-revolutionary the faubourgs of Paris come to the foreground; out of them new masses spring forward, the Sans-culottes. But what kind of people are they? Certainly there are wage-workers among them. But the majority were of a better class; there are traces of the trades out of which they had come or to which they yet belonged. The real mass of the Sans-culottes was not made out of wage-workers. It was rather the Parisian lower middle-class; it was, first, the guild-excluded master mechanics who dwelt in the Faubourg St. Antoine and Du Temple; secondly, the journeymen; thirdly, that element which the French call la boutique, retailers, tavern-keepers, etc., an important category. These, then, are the great hordes who clustered around Danton, Robespierre, and Marat. And what of these leaders themselves? Of what spirit are they children? They are, essentially, of the lower middle-class by birth. They are extreme radicals, extreme individualists. They are in their ideals and aims entirely unsocial and unproletarian according to our ideas to-day. The Constitution of 1793, in Article II., proclaims as Droits de l'Homme: Egalite, Liberte, Surete, Propriete. That is not proletarian and is not socialistic; thus all the assertions of a communistic movement at that time are thrown out. I have dwelt thus long on this revolution of 1793 in order to show how premature it is to speak of social democrats and of a social or proletarian movement wherever there is any outcry and disturbance.

I can but briefly touch upon other movements of this early history. The insurrection of Babeuf, 1796, bore certainly the communistic stamp; but, as we now know, it was without any response from the masses, who were finally tired of revolution.

Conspicuously of the upper middle-class were the July revolution of 1830 in France and the agitation of 1848 in Germany. In both cases we see citizenship in strife with feudal forces. Less clearly appears the civic character of the revolution of 1832 in England, and of the February revolution of 1848 in France, because these agitations were directed against forms of government sustained by citizens themselves. Yet even these movements, of 1832 in England and the February revolution in France, are not proletarian; they are rather the struggle of a part of the middle-class, the radicals, against another part, the Haute finance. This very opposition is now to be found again in Italy in the struggle of the North Italian industries against the rotten, half-feudal Haute finance which Crispi represents.

These are the agitations of our century which have been definite and conscious of their aim. In all of them the proletariat has been involved, behind all the barricades from 1789 to 1848 lie proletarian bodies; but of all those movements of which I have thus told you, not a single one is proletarian, or in our sense a social movement.

Where now the proletariat fights for itself and represents its own interests we discern at first mere muttered, inarticulate sounds; and it takes long for these tones to rise to cries, for these cries to grow to general demands, and to become crystallised into programmes. The first proletarian agitations-- movements of the unhappy, deeply buried mass--are, according to Carlyle's word, like the movements of Enceladus, who as he quivers in his pain causes an earthquake. These are movements of an entirely instinctive kind, claiming that which lies next, and attacking that which seems to them evidently to stand in the way. These are deeds which originally and largely assume the form of robbery and plunder. They have as their object to injure in some way the enemy in his power of possession. In England towards the close of the preceding and the beginning of the present century there was much destruction and plundering of manufactories. In the year 1812 the demolition of factories was punished in England with death, the best proof of the frequency of the fact. In other lands we have similar occurrences. I think of the factory-burning in Uster in Switzerland in the year 1832, of the weavers' riots in Germany in 1840, of the Lyons silk-weavers' insurrection in France in 1831. This last distinguishes itself from previous events of a similar character by the fact that it assumes as its great motive the motto which indeed we can think of as written over the portal of the proletarian movement: Vivre en travaillant, ou mourir en combattant! That is the first timid formulation of proletarian struggle, because the battle-cry is negatively and positively an expression of true proletarian-socialistic effort: negatively--no one shall live who does not work; positively--those who work shall be able to live. Thus this is the first development of proletarian agitation: attack upon the external and visible forms in which the opponent is incorporated--upon the manufactories and machines because in their coming lies competition with hand-work, upon the dwellings of the employers which appear as the citadels of the new dictators.

It is a step in advance when, in place of the immediate and visible object, there come into view the principles which lie behind these things, upon which the capitalistic system of economy rests--free competition in production. It is therefore advance in proletarian agitation as this begins to direct itself to the abolition of modern institutions. Thus the proletariat in England, towards the end of the previous and the beginning of the present century, struggled long for a revival of the Elizabethan trade law. This had specified that every master should have only one apprentice for three workmen. The time of apprenticeship should also be limited to seven years, the wages should be settled by a justice of the peace. This is an instinctive clutching after a protective barrier which seems to be disappearing. Even this is not at first clear; but essentially we find this trait common to all the antecedents of proletarianism, that the movements hold fast to what was in the good old times. Thus, for example, in Germany, the working-man's agitation of 1848 was largely an attempt to reintroduce the old guild system. But it all belongs to the antecedent history of the social movement, because there was no definite aim before the proletariat.

Also to this antecedent history belongs that great and well known movement, frequently specified as the first typical, socialistic-proletarian agitation; I mean the Chartist movement in England in 1837-1848. This differs from the brief outbreakings of the masses which we have just now specified in that it was carried on systematically for more than a decade, and it seems to us like a well organised movement. Without doubt it is a true proletarian agitation: if you wish so to call it, the first organised proletarian movement. It is proletarian because the great masses of the Chartists were of the labouring class; also, because its demands grew immediately out of the condition of the proletariat, and it exerted itself immediately for a material betterment of the oppressed factory-hands. Thus at that time the maximum day's work was presented as a demand; also, let me remind you of the celebrated phrase of the Rev. Mr. Stephens, who cried out to the masses: "The question which concerns us here is only one of knife and fork!" The Chartist movement is also proletarian because in it the antagonism between labour and capital arises often and sharply. The "government," the "ruling class," is identified with the capitalist. This finds expression in a genuine hate against employers which at that time possessed the masses and became a battle-cry. O'Connor's word, "Down with the wretches who drink the blood of our children, take pleasure in the misery of our wives, and become satiated by our sweat!" reminds us of the phraseology of the proletarian assemblages of the present day. Further, the demand for the right to work is thoroughly proletarian; so also the right to a full profit from the work, to the "increase" which flows into the pockets of the employer. A symptom of the proletarian character of the Chartist movement is seen in its growing indifference to political questions that do not immediately concern it; as, for example, concerning the abolition of the corn tax. It is interesting to see how gradually the Chartist movement became indifferent towards the most pressing interests of the middle-class; these, though originally included, were finally and completely thrown overboard. Also, in the form of the struggle we find the proletarian character. Thus, at that time the general strike appears as a means of warfare, an idea that can rise only in a true proletarian movement. So without doubt, for these and other reasons, we have in Chartism a proletarian agitation. But I place it in the antecedent history, because I miss in it the clear programme of the proletarian-social movement, a clearly defined aim towards which it works. The only programme of the Chartist movement is the charter, which contains no true socialistic postulates, but only a collection of parliamentary reforms. It is nothing other than a platform upon which a man stands because he knows nothing better; a programme that had been taken up by the radical middle-class democracy. It is O'Connell who transferred it to the proletariat: "universal suffrage, secret ballot, equal representation, payment for members of parliaments, no property qualifications for representatives, annual parliaments." Therefore, though the kernel of the Chartist movement seems to be proletarian and though the spirit which rules it is proletarian, it must be distinguished from later definite proletarian socialistic movements on account of the uncertainty of its platform. I speak thus emphatically, because frequently, even by such a distinguished student of English history as

Brentano, the Chartist is classed with the German social democrat. This conception holds too largely to the external form, which has similarity in both cases so far as these movements aspire after political power; but it is the inner character which is the determining feature of a social movement.

What characterises the antecedent history of the social movement everywhere is, as I have already said, its invariable similarity. Those agitations and exertions which I have specified as characteristic of the earlier history are invariably similar in every land, wherever we can speak of a social movement. But on the very threshold, in the passage from antecedent to present history, the differences in the social movements begin to become apparent. Unity at the beginning; diversity as the movement develops.

I distinguish three types; and for greater simplicity I call them the English, the French, and the German type. Under the English type of the working-man's movement I understand that agitation which has essentially an un-political, purely trade character. As the type of the French movement let me specify that which I call "revolutionism" or "Putschism," a kind of conspiracy coupled with street fights. And as the German type I would specify the lawful parliamentary-political working-man's agitation.

These are the three different forms in which the social movement now grows. In them all the living germs, which in general the social movement contains, unfold themselves to independent life, develop the peculiar and differing principles of this agitation. We shall see later that, after the different nations have developed their peculiarities, the social movement has a tendency again to greater uniformity.

* * * * *

Before we attempt to make clear these differences of national characteristics, it is perhaps well to settle a point which is decisive for a right understanding of the matter in general. I mean the main position which we as scientific observers should assume concerning this diversity of social movement. It is usual, as the variations of the movement are presented, to make a distinction between that which is called the healthy and normal on the one side, and the morbid movement on the other. Further, this distinction is usually identified with the difference between the movement in England and that upon the Continent. The English agitation, which is essentially a trade-union movement, they like to speak of as normal and proper; the Continental, which is rather political, as abnormal and improper. How shall we stand on this question? I believe that, in this discrimination and judgment, there is a twofold error, one of method and one of fact. When science pronounces any such judgment, entering into the realm of human history, that is in my opinion an overstepping of the bounds which a scientific man should place about himself. There is presented as objective knowledge a something that is purely subjective and merely the strong private opinion of an interested person--quite regardless of the fact that, as Hegel once expressed it, science always comes too late to teach a man how the world should be. So there lies here what I call a mistake of method. But this manner of looking at the matter involves also a mistake of fact, in that what it specifies as the normal tendency is the most abnormal that has ever existed, because the English social agitation could have become what it is only through a succession of unusual circumstances. For if we take the normal progress of modern capitalistic development as the objective standard of measurement, and in fact that is the only one which is of avail, then we would have much more right to say that the Continental movement is the normal, and the English the abnormal. I think, however, that it is more scientific to put aside the distinction between the normal and the abnormal, and to attempt rather to trace the causes for the different phases of the social movement in different lands. That at least shall be my attempt in what follows--to call attention to the variations of social movement, and to explain the reason for these variations in certain lands.

But what does it mean to "explain" these matters? Here also there is needed a word of definition, because in this, alas how often, we fail. Of course at this point we can say but little. To "explain" social occurrences means, naturally, to uncover the sources out of which they have sprung. It becomes necessary to trace these sources. And here we must not allow ourselves to become unrealistic, as is too often the case. I call any explanation of a social phenomenon unrealistic, which derives the fact superficially from the idealistic and altruistic motives of the persons involved, and which underestimates as impelling forces the preponderant interests of economic life, and which believes in miracles in the social world.

Thus, to make my point clear by an illustration, I hold that the usual explanation of the social development in England is unrealistic, that it cannot claim reality. According to this outline, matters in England have developed somewhat as follows: after the proletariat for some decades, and finally in the Chartist movement, had conducted itself in an unruly way in struggling for its interests, about the middle of this century it suddenly became polite, reconciled itself to the dominant economic order, and made peace with employers, who at the same time had become better men. All this occurred because a new spirit had come into man, a revolution of thought had occurred, a change from the individualistic and utilitarian view of things to a social conception of society and of the position and obligation of the individuals in it. The promoters and teachers of this new spirit are supposed to be, before all, Thomas Carlyle (1795-1881) and the Christian socialists Maurice, Kingsley, Ludlow, and others. Carlyle's teaching culminates in sentences like these: The evils which have broken out over Europe--the French Revolution!--Chartism!--rest upon this, that the spirit of evil rules; mammonism, selfishness, forgetfulness of obligation. This spirit must be reformed; faith instead of scepticism, idealism instead of mammonism, self-sacrifice instead of selfishness, and social spirit instead of individualism must again come into the heart of man. The individual must not be the central point, as is the case in the eudemonistic-utilitarian philosophy; but social aims, objective work, ideals, shall direct the activity of man. From this conception of the fulfilment of social obligation the relation between the proletariat and the capitalist becomes ennobled and its harshness is relieved; the employer must become humanised, learn to rule truly; the workman must become manageable, learn to serve truly. Quite similarly reason the so-called Christian socialists, save that they would derive the "new social spirit" from the teachings of Christianity.

These teachings are said to bring forth fruit. That social spirit--who would have thought it!--does in fact, they say, enter into the hearts of men; the social conflict is hereby removed from the world; in place of hate and mistrust enter love and confidence. The "social question" is solved; at least we are upon the way to "social peace," capitalism is saved, socialism is sloughed off.

I shall investigate later the extent to which the social facts, here asserted, can claim reality; but assuming this--that pure harmony rules in Albion--can such a hyper-idealistic explanation satisfy us? Must we not introduce some more substantial causes than merely the results of Carlyle's sermons?

Absolute proof of the one or the other conception, naturally, cannot be had, because it is the critic's philosophy, his estimate of man, that finally decides; Wallenstein the realist and Max the idealist can never fully convince one another. Anyone can, through a massing of reasons and proofs, make the truth of his assertion concerning certain evident facts at least plausible.

I, for my part, am sceptical concerning all optimistic explanations of history, and believe rather with Wallenstein than with Max. And as now, forced by this ill-favoured mistrust, I look more closely at the development in England of the matter that lies before us, I get a picture essentially different from that which I have sketched for you as the prevailing conception. Before all, I find but little of that renowned "social spirit," which is said to have accomplished such wonders. In the institutions which are characteristic of proletarian development in England, trade-unions and brotherhoods, rules, so far as I can see, a healthy spirit of selfishness. Perhaps there is no social creation which is built more brutally upon selfishness than the trade-union--necessarily so. And as I read the troubled outpourings of the Christian socialists over the complete failure of their exertions, I can bring them easily into harmony with other observations. But even allowing that there is a certain effectiveness of the "social spirit," that it does exist, shall I believe that it is able to remove mountains? Or shall I not venture to assume that the economic and political development, controlled by selfishness, has strongly helped, has created the conditions in which the social spirit could work?

All this I present in a kindly spirit. My conclusion is that I cannot possibly be satisfied with Carlyle and his "social spirit," but must seek a realistic explanation, for England as for other lands. And this is indeed not difficult. Let us see how the national peculiarities of the social movement, considering the actual facts of history, can be understood as the necessary results of specific lines of development.

CHAPTER IV

THE DEVELOPMENT OF NATIONAL PECULIARITIES

"Die Staaten (und) Voelker ... in diesem Geschaefte des Weltgeistes stehen in ihrem besonderen bestimmten Principe auf, das an ihrer Verfassung und der ganzen Breite ihres Zustandes seine Auslegung und Wirklichkeit hat, deren sie sich bewusst und in deren Interesse vertieft, sie zugleich bewustlose Werkzeuge und Glieder jenes inneren Geschaefts sind, worin diese Gestalten vergehen, der Geist an und fuer sich aber sich den Uebergang in seine naechste hoehere Stufe vorbereitet und erarbeitet."--HEGEL, Rechtsphilosophie, Sec. 344.

How shall we now, in a word, characterise the English working-men's movement? I think thus: since 1850 the definitely "revolutionary" agitation has ceased--that is, the working-men's movement accepts the bases of the capitalistic order of society, and endeavours through the establishment of benevolent funds, brotherhoods, and trade-unions, within the existing economy, to improve the condition of the working man. The opposition of classes is lessened; the worker is recognised as a man both by society and by his employer. Doubtless an elevation of the English working-class is accomplished. Effective legislation for the protection of the working man is secured; concerning which I would remark incidentally that this "elevation" tends in fact only to an aristocracy of working men such that, for example, in London immeasurable misery results--over 100,000 persons in that city are supported by the poor-rates, $25,000,000 are yearly disbursed in charity, one-fifth of the deaths occur in almshouses, public hospitals, etc. But not to dwell on this; other strata of the English proletariat have without doubt considerably improved their condition.

And now to the point;--all this is without part taken by the working man in politics, without the assumption of a political character by the working-men's movement, without constituting an independent working-men's party.

As we seek for the causes of such development, immediately we notice that, whether or not the "social spirit" has helped, we cannot think of this trait without considering a most peculiar combination of political and economic circumstances in England from 1850 to about 1880.

Without doubt the position of industrial monopoly which England reached, and which gave a tremendous economic impulse to the nation, was the solid basis of all social development. A few figures in illustration.

The railroads of the United Kingdom covered

in 1842--1,857 English miles, in 1883--18,668 English miles.

The ships entering all British harbours amounted

in 1842 to 935,000 tons, in 1883 to 65,000,000 tons.

The import and export business was valued

in 1843 at about L103,000,000, in 1883 at about L732,000,000.

This means that the other nations could not rival England in extending the market for an increasing productiveness. It betokens a remarkable infrequence of disturbance through financial crises and market stagnation.

From this come important consequences for the working man: a generally favourable condition of the labour market, constantly growing need of labour, less lack of work, on the one side; on the other, satisfaction of the employer, and his inclination and ability to remunerate better the workman, to give him some share in the golden stream of profit.

Besides this peculiar combination of circumstances of an economic nature, which can never again come to any land because the competing and strengthened nations now struggle for supremacy in the markets of the world, consider the most remarkable condition of political party life in England.

It is well known that this rests, at least since the beginning of this century, upon an alternation of power between the two great parties, the Tories and the Whigs. They both strive after control, and they reach this from time to time by shrewd concession, to the spirit of progress, by a happy use of the situation at the moment. Now one, now the other, quickly seizes and masters it. The tertius gaudens in this struggle for mastery is the working men as a class. It does not require much penetration to see that, for example, the radical English legislation in favour of the working man has come to pass only through the spite of the Tories, agrarian in their interests, against the liberal manufacturers. But if you wish to suppose noble motives for parliamentary majorities, the resolution of the Tories to provide protection for the industrial proletariat must at least have been made easy through the consideration that the land proletariat would never get such laws. Later, especially since extension of the franchise, the policy of the Whigs was directed to reaching rule, or to sustaining themselves therein, with the help of the working man. That involved, naturally, concessions and a spirit of friendliness to the working class, even if hard to yield, even if the employers had not personal interest in these concessions.

But the employers--thanks again to the happy combination of circumstances at that time in England--had without doubt to some degree a direct and personal interest, if not in advancing, at least in not opposing, the exertions of the working class for an improvement of their situation within the limits of the existing economic order.

Thus gradually the trade unions and their regulations were recognised by the employers: the latter declared themselves ready to deal conclusively with the representatives of the workmen, and took part in arbitrations, conciliations, etc. Was this only out of consideration for the workman? Was it really because Carlyle had so advised? Was it not rather merely out of purely selfish motives? Was it not that the conservative, aristocratic trade-unions were a bulwark against all tendency to revolution, sure and strong as no police regulation could erect? And because methods of agreement offered a useful means of avoiding strikes and the consequent disturbances of trade, which were extremely feared because business was always favourable, and because every day they could make money, and because every day in which the manufactory stood still a considerable lucrum cessans was involved?

And, finally, why should not legislation in favour of the working man be recommended? Even if the cost of production is somewhat increased, we are easily in position to recover the charge from the consumer. But production is not necessarily made more costly; the shortening of the hours of labour can be made good through an increased intensity of work, and thereby arises an advantage in having capable workmen, who are gradually paid at higher rates. Or this drawback may be counterbalanced by improvement of machinery; this they were the more willing to do, for capital was abundant, and no bounds would be placed to increase of production and sale by the possibilities of the market. Lastly, they would remember that shrewd legislation in favour of the working-man is an excellent weapon for the large concerns to use against the small, in order to do away with the disagreeable competition of petty manufacturers. But all this is with the assurance that an expansion of production will not be hindered, but rather be demanded, by the condition of the market.

But now, granting that all could be accomplished in so easy and business-like a way, as the social evolution in England has, in fact, been accomplished under the said conditions, we must consider, in addition, the peculiar temperament of the English working-man. Because he is such a moderate and practical fellow, he is fitted for any policy that does not oblige him to see beyond his nose; and he is satisfied with it. "Always something practical," is his motto; his social-political "business," as his yarn and iron business, has nothing of the elan of the French, of the subtle thought of the German, of the fire of the Italian workman.

This practical tendency finds its true incorporation in the old English trade-union, which, as I have already said, is the shrewdest scheme for the protection of personal interests that has ever been conceived; diplomatic, adroit, smooth towards that which is above--towards the employer; exclusive, narrow, brutal towards that which is underneath--towards four-fifths of the "outsiders," the poorer classes of workmen. The trade unions are capitalistic and business-like organisations, which the calculating practical sense of the English working-man has infused with his spirit. Hence, surely in great part, their large results.

Such causes as these seem to me at the bottom of the social development of England from 1850 to 1880. It was the coincidence of a number of circumstances favourable to capital that produced this business-like organisation of the working man--that specific type which we call English.

Thus there is no socialism, no social movement in the strict sense of the term, no struggle of classes; but there is a "social peace," or at least an approach towards such, upon the basis of the capitalistic economy.

Is it truly "social peace"? Perhaps it is only a postponement of the struggle. It seems almost so; unless all signs fail, this "social peace" will not last much longer in England. Since the passing of English supremacy from the markets of the world, since the rise of lower strata of working men, the "social movement" is again on. The sense of solidarity throughout the proletariat awakens anew. With it comes the strife of classes. The question of independent political action on the part of the working man now stands as a matter of discussion before the working-men's congresses. Already have socialistic theories and demands made impression upon the orthodox membership of the trade unions. But of this we must not here speak. I would merely refer to the fact that the time from 1850 to 1880 is rightly called the period of social truce; it was the time in which the specific English type of the working-man's movement was developed.

There is no doubt that, even if this in its peculiar form gradually disappears, it will be of continued influence upon the further development of the social movement. What the English working-man has left as a lasting inheritance to the agitation of the proletariat consists of rich experiences in the sphere of trade-unionism, and a steadiness, a calm, a business-like clearness of procedure on the part of organised labour. It is, in a word, the method of agitation that comes over from the English type and will remain in the proletariat, even if the direction of agitation becomes essentially different.

And now we leave British ground. Now we step over the Channel, and go into France. What a change of scene! Out of foggy, smoky England, with its earnest, capable, dull populace, into the charming, sunny, warm land of France, with its passionate, impulsive, hasty population.

What kind of a social movement is this in France? I have already given some indications. All ferments and boils there, all bubbles and breaks out uninterruptedly since the "glorious" revolution of the previous century. Parties are in a state of constant flux; a movement divides itself into countless factions. With haste and pressure single acts fall over one another. Parliamentary struggle is set aside, now by bloody street fights, now by conspiracy, now by assassination. To understand clearly this general characteristic, which runs to-day in the very blood of the French proletariat, but which is becoming modified, we must go back to the earlier decades. We must think of the activity of the clubs and companies of conspirators in the third and fourth decades of this century; we must recall the awful street fights which the Parisian proletariat waged with heroism in the June days of the year 1848, and, later, in the May days of the year 1871. There is, as it were, a smouldering, inner fire that glows constantly in the masses and their leaders, and that, when any nourishment comes to it, breaks out violently and devastates all around. The social movement in France has always had in it something morbid, excited, convulsive. Mighty, magnificent, in sudden outbreaks; again faint and flagging after the first repulse. Always looking forward, always with inspiration; but often fantastic, dreamy, uncertain in its choice of ways and means. But always filled with a faith in quick accomplishment, in sudden action, whether with the ballot or with the dagger; always filled with faith in the miracle of revolution. In this I present its motto: the characteristic of the French type lies in the word "revolutionism"-- by which I mean belief in revolution-making. Involved in this revolutionism lie all the other peculiarities, as seed-corn in the sheath. Let me specify them-- pardon some of the harsh word-making! Factionism, clubbism, and Putschism. Factionism is the tendency to separate into innumerable small parties; clubbism is the desire of conspiracy in secret companies and conventicles; Putschism, finally, is the fanatical tendency towards street struggle, faith in the barricade.

Whence all this? One thing springs immediately to the attention of the student of French history: what we here have learned to recognise as a characteristic trait of the movement of the French proletariat is to be found almost without change in all the actions of the French middle-classes. Indeed, it is evidently an inheritance that the proletariat has assumed. Unnoticeably the one movement passes into the other. The French proletariat is led into history by the hand of the bourgeoisie. Long after the proletariat in France had begun an independent agitation, the influence of this former movement was conspicuous. Not only in the method of strife; as well in the programmes and ideals of the French proletariat, this middle-class spirit stands even to our latest time, so that we can understand why Proudhon, the greatest theorist of the revolutionary movement, as late as after 1848 had influence in the circles of the French proletariat. That Proudhon was really a bourgeois theorist is often denied, but is none the less true; however revolutionary his phraseology may be, all his proposals for reform--whether the exchange and credit banks, or the wage theory, or the "establishment of value,"--point to an upholding, a strengthening, an ethicizing of individualistic production and the exchange of individual service.

But no one who looks at the matter will wonder at the long predominance of middle-class influence in the French proletarian movement. What prestige the French, especially the Parisian, middle-class has won in the eyes of the populace, in the course of later French history! How many chaplets of fame have been laid upon its brow since the days of 1793! In no other land, Italy perhaps excepted, has it proved itself so valiant, daring, successful. If the French bourgeoisie, as no other in the world, has made a free path for itself in so short a time through the overcoming of feudal institutions, truly the iron broom of Napoleon has done a great share of this work. But we must not forget that it is the revolution of 1793--the uprising of the middle class--which has levelled the ground; that is the historic significance of the Reign of Terror, and with it of the middle-class that since those days has borne an aureole upon its head.

But it is not only this rather ideal element that is responsible for the preponderance of the middle-class influence in France; we must add the weighty fact that a great part of the specifically French industries, owing to the peculiar organisation in ateliers, bears a half-individualistic character, and that these are largely industries of the arts. Thus the Lyons silk industry and many of the Parisian manufactures of luxury. These are in sharp contrast, for example, to the great English staple industries of coal, iron, and cotton. The French ouvrier, in Lyons directly called maitre ouvrier, assumes, through the tendency and organisation of many French industries, a more individualistic, and so middle-class, appearance than the proletariat in other lands.

But to understand the characteristics which are stamped upon the social movement in France as an inheritance from the middle-class, to explain that enthusiasm for revolution of which I have spoken to you, we must look at the whole history of France. That people!--a sanguine, enthusiastic race, with a volatile temperament, with a dash which is not to be found in those of northern lands. Perhaps the French type of the social movement, somewhat modified by German influence, is again to be found in Italy; there we must learn to see its peculiar characteristics, the quick response of large masses, the straw fire of momentary enthusiasm--in short, we must understand clearly an entirely different mode of thought and feeling in order to comprehend this French, or, if you will, Roman, type of the born revolutionist, in its heaven-wide difference from the English workman. Victor Hehn says somewhere, in his striking way, concerning the Italians, but it can be applied to all of the Latin races:

"Completely strange to him is the German, and even more so the English!--Philistine, quite unthinkable, is the temperament of those unimaginative and well-meaning sons of habit who, arrayed with all the virtues of the commonplace, are respectable through the moderation of their claims, are slow in comprehension, ... and who drag after them throughout their lives, with pathetic patience, a burden of social prejudices received from their fathers."

Thus one of Latin race strives after a far-off object, and does not shrink from forceful means of reaching it. This heaven-storming temperament has been given to him by nature for his mission in history. Further, in order to understand the character of the social movement in France, think of the preponderance in this land of the capital city, Paris! If Paris is not exactly France, as is often asserted, yet it is strong enough to dictate on occasion the laws of the people. Paris, this nerve ganglion! This rumbling volcano!

Further, I have always the impression that the French people stand even to-day under the influence, perhaps we may say the ban, of their "glorious" revolution. The influence of such an event--the most tremendous drama of history--cannot in one hundred years disappear from a people. So I think that this nervosity, if I may so express it, which clings to all public life in France, may be, in large part, a heritage from those terrible years of general overthrow, an inheritance that has been most carefully fostered in less glorious revolutions since then--ah, how many! And out of that time springs something else: an overmastering faith in force, in the availability of the political riot. The history of France has developed itself since the July days of 1789 rather from without to within, than from within to without; the change of regime has played a mighty role, has often worked decisively upon the progress of social life. It is not strange that always they rest their hope upon it, and seek to use further, as a means of development, the political revolution which has often wrought so mightily. This belief in revolution stands, however, in close connection, I think, with the specifically French, optimistic, ideal-socialistic philosophy of the eighteenth century, of which I have heretofore spoken. In France is the classic ground of that belief in the ordre naturel, which can come over the world "as a thief in the night," because it is already here and needs only to be uncovered.

If, now, we would see all of the innumerable influences that work together in order to produce the peculiar type of French agitation, we must notice that in this land a strange growth of modern times has struck deep root-- anarchism. For centuries past preparations had been made for its easy entrance. For what is anarchism fundamentally other than a new form of pure revolutionism in method, of middle-class ideals as object? Are not Ravachol and Caserio the true sons of those conspirators who inspired the France of 1830 and 1840? Is there any more legitimate father of anarchy than Blanqui? Anarchy, we may say, is born of the marriage of the social philosophy of the eighteenth century with the revolutionism of the nineteenth; it is a bloody renaissance of social utopism.

Here mention must be made of a matter which I have carefully avoided thus far, because it is an hypothesis which I must lay before you with a question-mark. Has the fact that the land is divided among so many small owners had any effect upon the peculiar development of the modern anarchistic movement? I mean, there must be a connection between both these phenomena. Indeed, it is a question as to how far anarchism has ever obtained in the masses. But, so far as I can see, wherever the anarchistic propaganda seems to spread it is always in agrarian districts; I recall the work of Bakunin in Italy and Spain, and, as well, the nestling of anarchism now again in France. And wherever the country people have been aroused to independent agitation, this movement has always shown at least a trace of anarchism. For examples, Italy and Spain and Ireland.

It is an interesting problem:--Is, and if so, why is, anarchy the theoretical expression of agrarian revolution? The investigation of this would lead away from my present purpose, which is to speak of the proletarian-socialistic agitation. But I would at least present it.

If you ask me, finally, what lasting effect the peculiarity of the French agitation has had upon the great international movement of the proletariat, I answer--perhaps the least of all the nations, since it bears unmistakable marks of unripeness. But I believe that it will be the model for all other races, because of the idealism, the elan, the energy, which distinguish it from the movements of other nations. I wonder if the proletariat in Paris may not again be filled with an inspiration for some ideal, while we middle-class citizens of other nations are in danger of decadence!

You all know what wonderful progress the proletarian movement has made in Germany. For as we look back to the inconsiderable beginnings about the year 1840--they were rather agitation by hand-workers than true proletarian disturbances--suddenly, in the year 1863, as if shot out of a pistol, appears an independent political working-men's party, not again to disappear, but to grow to mighty proportions.

Whence comes this strange apparition of such a social agitation in Germany? How can we explain the suddenness of its entrance, and especially the fundamental traits of its character--its legal-parliamentary tendency, and its self-reliance from the beginning even until now?

At first we may incline to the thought that the causes for the peculiarities of agitation in Germany should be sought in the personality of its founder, Ferdinand Lassalle. Without doubt we owe much to the individuality of this extraordinary man. We know what kind of a fire it was that burnt consumingly within him--a demoniacal ambition, a Titanic eagerness for fame. And as this ambition, after many years of scientific renown, finally led him into the sphere of politics, wherein all ambitious men who cannot be generals and artists in our time must necessarily go, it was only natural that the masterful Lassalle should become leader, chief, prince. Where Bismarck stood, another could stand only in the shadow; but the opposition would not have Lassalle--apparently about 1855-1865 he desired to ally himself with them, but they feared this man to whom they would not yield themselves. There remained only one thing, to become the leader of a new and distinct party, the working-men's party. This was Lassalle's party in the strictest sense, his hammer, his sword, with which he would win for himself a position in political life.

But these personal elements must be aided by circumstances, the specific conditions of political and social life in Germany, in order to crown Lassalle's efforts with success and to establish thoroughly the movement during the short year of his leadership.

I will not here dwell much upon the German national characteristics. Concerning the peculiarities of the English and the French types of the social movement this was necessary; but the German type owes little to racial character. We dwell rather upon the external, incidental circumstances in order to explain the peculiarities of the social movement in Germany; and it is not hard to trace the chain of causes.

In Germany a real revolutionary movement, like that in France, was not at this time possible--even if we assume that German character would thus incline. The opportunity came too late. Revolutionism in the French sense bears, as I have already said, the mark of unripeness. Revolutionism may influence a nation long, but it cannot be made the ruling motive of a social movement at so late a point of time as that at which the German agitation began because the stage of unripeness has passed. Take for example Italy, whose people certainly by nature tend towards revolutionism; yet they must conform to the experiences of older lands even if the inner nature always urges to outbreak.

On the other hand, Germany, as its social agitation began, was yet so immature economically--like England at the end of the last century--that the subordination of economic to political agitation is easily understood.

But would it not have been perhaps more natural if the proletariat, when it desired to enter into a legal-parliamentary course of action, had sought alliance with the existing party of opposition--as has happened in other lands? We must lay stress on the fact that it was hindered in this through the incapacity of the middle-class party of that time in radical politics; for this reason it could not at the time absorb the proletariat.

It is a part of the inheritance which German liberalism has received from the year 1848 that one of its chief characteristics is the fear of the red spectre--revolution. Indeed the proletariat has itself helped towards this by its behaviour. We all know how the middle-class agitation of the year 1848 in Germany failed, and sought the protection of the Prussian bayonet from the "gens mal intentionnes"--the well-known undercurrent of democracy present in every civil revolution. Civic pride and defiance fell at that moment, as always, when the spectre of social revolution appeared on the horizon--witness the law against the socialists. Thus was the bridge between the proletarian agitation and civic opposition even at that early time broken, soon to be entirely destroyed.

As in the strictly political sphere this fear and hesitation did not permit the liberal party to come to decided radicalism, which probably would have contented the proletariat for a long time, so in the economic sphere earlier German liberalism was characterised by what we to-day would call an incomprehensible doctrinairism, an inane obsession derived from the dreary Manchester school of thought. The exertions of Schulze-Delitzsch, who was indeed in his sphere a serviceable man, could not nearly make good the shortcomings of the liberal party in all questions of social politics. The liberal political economists of that time had no understanding of the demands and movements of the proletariat. Such pitiful writings on the so-called "working-man's question" as those by Prince-Smith are not produced by writers of reputation in other lands, so far as I know. Possibly this or that great man de l'Institut has rivalled them.

The inability of the liberal party to draw the gushing water of proletarian agitation to its own mill finds striking example in the answer which, in the year 1862, a deputation of working-men from Leipsic received from the leaders of the "National Union." The working men had applied for the privilege of taking part in political life. They wanted some recognition for their leaders. And what was given as answer? That the working men were by birth already honorary members of the union!

And now Bismarck, in spite of the fact that the liberal party was refusing the franchise to the proletariat, forced upon the country in the year 1867 a universal, direct, and secret ballot, a bequest of Lassalle's. We are tempted to assume diabolical revenge against the liberals as a motive for this. For the moulding of the social movement in Germany this had two consequences of fundamental importance. First, it weakened yet more the middle class, which, now between the aristocracy and the proletariat, was sinking into an ever-increasing insignificance and, through fear of the growing working-men's party, lost more and more of its self-confidence. Hence a further estrangement between the liberal party and the proletarian movement ensued.

Secondly, this franchise that had fallen into the lap of the working man inclined the leaders of the proletariat to purely parliamentary agitation, and for a long time hindered them from a right understanding of the non-political aims of the proletariat.

We may look upon all this with sorrow or with joy--and everyone who sympathises with the fate of his people will feel in one way or the other; now we must accept it as a fact, the existence of which cannot be changed, even if for the future we alter the particular objects of political effort. But the purpose of science is only to explain how things have unfolded themselves; and only that is the idea which has ruled throughout this my work. Hut of course there are always people unable to separate science and politics.

One remark in conclusion! This Lassalle movement, and with it also the German type of social agitation, bears the stamp not only of historic-national interest, as I have attempted to show to you, but also much of purely personal characteristics; as is proved by the mysticism, the cult of a person and the creation of a sect, to which the movement has deteriorated. Has it never occurred to you how remarkable it is that this movement, perhaps more than any other, has developed, in spite of its German and personal characteristics, into a world-wide and enduring "school," if I may so express it? Of this there can be no doubt.

One ground for this may be found in the personality of its creator, in the passionate force of his oratory, in the power of his agitation. Treitschke thinks that Germany has possessed three great agitators, List, Blum, and Lassalle. Surely Lassalle is the greatest leader of the proletariat thus far; the only agitator of real greatness which the proletariat has thus far had. For this reason his personality continues in force even until now.

"In Breslau a churchyard--a dead man in grave: There slumbers the one who to us the sword gave."

But here again we are not satisfied with the purely personal element; we must rather seek after the real grounds for the explanation of the fact.

To me it seems that the triumph of the German type in the international movement, as it was begun through Lassalle, lies essentially in the circumstance that Lassalle's agitation, and then the later German movement, is filled by the spirit of that man who was called to formulate the theories which should bring to a sharp point all the general objects of proletarian effort. You know that I mean Karl Marx.

The name of this man expresses all the centripetal force which the modern social movement contains. From him comes all that which tends to remove national peculiarities and to make an international movement. "Marxism" is the tendency to make the social movement international, to unify it. But of this we must not here speak; only of its peculiar features. The one great social movement runs first into separate streams of national effort; later these unite again. There is throughout a tendency to return to unity. But the movement develops itself in national lines and is determined by contingencies which make history. The general law of these incidental circumstances I have tried to show to you to-day.

And now at last let us pass to the theorist of the social movement, Karl Marx.

CHAPTER V

KARL MARX

"+Ktema es aei.+"

THUC., i., 22.

Karl Marx was born in Treves in the year 1818, the son of a Jewish lawyer, who was later baptised into the Christian faith. Intelligence and general culture were at home in the house of his parents. The favourite authors of the family were Rousseau and Shakespeare, the latter of whom was the favourite poet of Karl Marx throughout life. An element of cosmopolitanism was conspicuous in the household life of the Marx family. Their closest intercourse was with the family von Westphalen, the parents of the later Prussian minister--the half-Scottish, highly cultured Baron Edgar. To this man the young Karl owed his first introduction to literature, and later to his wife Jenny.

Karl studied philosophy and history in Bonn, purposing to become a Prussian professor. By the year 1842 he came to the point of formal admission as lecturer. But difficulties soon presented themselves; the young Marx, then allied with Bruno Bauer, was carried away by the reactionary tendency which at that time swept again over the Prussian universities, especially over heretical Bonn. As customarily happens in such cases of aborted career, the young Marx became a journalist. Soon he emigrated, because in 1844 the Prussian police drove him out of the land; he fled to Paris, was thrown out again by Guizot on demand, we suppose, of Prussia; in 1845 he went to Brussels, returning to Germany during the year 1848; finally after the year 1849 he found rest in London from the pressure of the police. Here he lived until his death in the year 1883.

His personality, the characteristics of which were strikingly developed through the external circumstances of his life, was marked by extraordinary intellectual activity. He was a pitiless and positive critic in his very nature. He had an abnormally sharp vision for psychological and historical continuity, especially where these are based upon the less noble impulses of mankind. A word of Pierre Leroux's seems to me as if coined for Marx: "il etait ... fort penetrant sur le mauvais cote de la nature humaine." So it was by nature easy for him to believe in Hegel's teaching that "evil" has accomplished all the development of mankind. His conception of the world is expressed in Wallenstein's magnificent words:

"To the bad spirit belongs the earth, not to the good; the good things that the gods send to us from above are to be held only in communal possession. Their light gives us joy, yet makes no man rich; in their kingdom there is no private possession."

What qualified Karl Marx to reach the first rank among the social philosophers of the nineteenth century, and to obtain next to Hegel and Darwin the greatest influence upon modern ideas, was the fact that he united a knowledge of the highest form of the historic philosophy of his time--Hegel--with a knowledge of the highest form of social life--that of Western Europe, of France, and especially of England. It was because he knew how to concentrate, as by a lens, all the rays of light which had been shed by other thinkers, and because he was able through his cosmopolitan experience to withdraw attention from the incidental features of national development, and to concentrate it upon what is typical in modern social life.

Marx, in common with his friend Friedrich Engels, in a large number of monographs, the best known of which is Capital, has laid the ground-lines of an amazing system of social philosophy; but this is not the place for a study of its particular features. What interests us much more at this time is the Marxian theory of social agitation, because this is especially what has enabled him to influence decisively the progress of social development. In no single book of his is this theory comprehensively presented. Yet we find all the essential elements of it in the celebrated "Communistic Manifesto" of Marx and Engels in the year 1847, which was presented as a programme to the "League of the Righteous" in Brussels; they accepted it and thus changed themselves into a "League of Communists." The "Communistic Manifesto" contained the principles of a philosophy of history, upon which the programme of a party is based. Its leading thoughts are these:

All history is the story of a struggle between classes; the history of the present is the story of the struggle between the middle class and the proletariat. The making of classes results from certain economic conditions of production and distribution, through which also social control is determined. "Immanent" forces (the expression does not occur in the "Communistic Manifesto," but becomes later a technical term) constantly revolutionise the conditions of production, and thus of all economic matters. In our time this organic change is accomplished with especial quickness, because the tremendous forces of production created by the middle class grow too fast. Thus on the one side the conditions of existence under the present capitalistic economy quickly deteriorate; upon the other side the conditions of existence tend to a social organisation without classes upon a basis of common production and communal ownership of the means of production (this formula, also, is not found in the "Communistic Manifesto," in which merely the abolition of private property is presented; but our phrase first occurs two years later, in the history of class struggle in France). This deterioration appears in the crises in which society feels itself "suddenly thrown back into a condition of momentary barbarism," and in the emergence of pauperism in which it plainly appears now

"that the middle class is unfit longer to remain the ruling class of society and to enforce the life condition of itself as the ruling law; it is unfit to rule because it is incapable of securing subsistence to its slave within the terms of his slavery, because it is compelled to let him sink into a position in which it must support him instead of being supported by him."

But the conditions of the new social order (this thought also is merely suggested in the "Communistic Manifesto" and only later, especially by Engels, is it developed) are created by an enormous increase of the forces of production and by the "communisation of the processes of production" which goes hand in hand with this increase--that is, the interweaving and combination of the individual acts of production, and transition to co-operative methods, etc.

The most important consequence now for our question is this: the economic revolution finds its spontaneous expression in opposition and struggle of classes, the "modern social movement"--that is, the movement of the proletariat is nothing but the organisation of those elements of society which are called to break the rule of the middle class and "to conquer the new social forces of production." This they can accomplish only by "abolishing their own private appropriation as it has thus far existed and with it the whole idea of private property"; that is, in place of private possession and private production to establish communism.

The "communists"--that is, the political party for which the "Communistic Manifesto" serves as a confession of faith--are only a part of the warring proletariat; they form that part which is conscious of the process of development. This party "distinguishes itself from the other proletarian elements only in that on the one side it emphasises and enforces in the different national campaigns of the proletariat the interests of the proletariat as a whole, and on the other hand in that in the different stages of development through which the struggle between the proletariat and the bourgeoisie passes, invariably it represents the interests of the general proletarian movement."

"The theories of the communists rest in no way upon ideas or principles which have been discovered by this or that reformer. They are only general expressions of the actual conditions in an existing struggle of classes, an agitation which is happening historically before our very eyes."

The thoughts here expressed, as I have already indicated in several places in this review, have been later to some extent more precisely worded, have been to some decree enlarged and developed, have been in part modified; but the ground-lines of Marx's theory of the social movement are already revealed in them all. In what now lies their historic importance? How shall we explain their tremendous power of conquest? Whence comes their continuance already through a half-century?--and all this, in spite of the fact that, as I believe, this theory errs in essential points, and that it can scarcely indeed sustain itself as a whole!

Before I now attempt to give the answer I must make one thing clear. What Marx and Engels have left to us as an intellectual inheritance, whether we consider their writings from 1842, or even only those after 1847, seems at first as if it were a confused mass of varied thought-material. Only he who looks closely and who takes the trouble to enter into the spirit of the men can bring the separated lines of thought into order. Such an one finds that some fundamental ideas run through the writings of Marx and Engels during the whole period of their literary activity; also that at different times quite different lines of thought run across and confuse the system which, as a whole, is built up upon these great ideas. Most exponents of the Marxian teaching, especially those representing the middle class, have made the mistake of not separating the essential from the accidental, and have as a result not been able to do justice to the historic significance of these theories. Naturally it is easier to start with the contradictions and inconsistencies of an author, rather than to make tedious tracing of what is of lasting worth; it is easy, but not right, to content oneself with detached and apparent blunders and mistakes in the teaching of an important thinker, in order to reject this teaching in toto. Marxism, as no other teaching, offers itself for such treatment; partly because many of his theories awake the passions of the critic and hence must in advance prevent calm judgment, partly because in fact, as already said, it presents a most clumsy confusion of contradictory teachings. This is shown in the fact that even now, after his thoughts have lived through a half-century, we must still exert ourselves to get at the real meaning and the deep importance of his teaching. This is due especially to the "middle-class" critics of Marx; but it is also because of the members of his own party. I recall the fact that the fundamental principle of Marx's economic system--the theory of value--has become an object of fruitful discussion as lately as two years ago. At that time I attempted to bring into use this method which I have just specified as the only true one for such a peculiar formation as the Marxian teaching; I asked how the parts of Marx's theory which stand in such opposition to each other could be reconciled, in order to bring out the sense which so earnest a thinker must surely have laid underneath. At that time the aged Engels could bear witness that I had about "hit the right mark," but that he could not endorse all that I had "introduced" into the Marxian teaching. Other critics thought at the time that nothing more would be heard of Marx's teaching concerning value. Perhaps they are right; but if Marx's Theory of Value is a scientific work, it can be such only in my interpretation.

I have thus spoken in order to show you how I stand concerning Marx's theory of the social movement. I make most earnest effort to separate it from all extraneous matter, to comprehend it in its essential points, and so to present these essentials in such way that they shall be consistent with reality. At the same time I emphasise the spirit of Marx's theories, and only hope that it is truly the soul of Marx, and not of myself, "in which the times reflect themselves."

I shall attempt to speak later concerning what I look upon as confusing "non-essentials" of the theory; I speak now of what I think to be the historically important essence--the +ktema es aei+--of Marx's theory of the social movement.

First and before all, it is a scientific accomplishment of the first order to give prominence to the historic conception of the social movement and the inner relationship of the "economic," "social," and "political" manifestations and precedents. Marx applies the evolution idea to the social movement. Other conspicuous men have tried to consider socialism and the social movement as in the flow of historic life--I think, for example, of Lorenz von Stein, that writer who, perhaps, has most influenced Marx. But no one has so clearly, illuminatively, effectively shown these historical relations. That political revolutions and agitations are fundamentally great displacements of social classes is a truth enunciated before the time of Marx; but no one has ever presented it in so impressive a way. He takes economic revolutions as his starting-point, in order to explain the creation and the conflict of social classes; and in Misere (175), before the "Communistic Manifesto," he had already said: "il n'y a jamais de mouvement politique qui ne soit social en meme temps." But therewith--and it is this that is of importance to us--is the proletariat brought to full self-consciousness and taught to know itself in its historic relations. Out of this historic conception arises, for Marx and for the proletariat, with certainty the main points of the programme and the tactics of the social movement. They are only "a general expression of actual relations in an existing struggle of classes," as the "Communistic Manifesto" has expressed it somewhat vaguely. To state it more exactly, the theory of Marx affirms the identification of that which unconsciously and instinctively had arisen as a proletarian idea with that which is actually observable as the result of economic development. As to tactical management, however, the idea was decisive that revolutions could not be forced, but were the outgrowth of specific economic antecedents; while class strife in both its forms--the political, of which the "Communistic Manifesto" speaks chiefly, and the economic, for which in Misere Marx breaks a lance--is recognised as the instrument which the proletariat must use in order to protect its interests during the process of economic transformation. Thus he formulates that which every intelligent proletarian movement must recognise as its fundamental principles. Socialism as a goal, struggle between classes as the way towards it, cease to be merely personal opinions, and are understood as necessary.

This elementary conception, that these two main pillars of the modern social movement are not merely arbitrary creations, but are unavoidable products of the historic development, is even to-day so little accepted that it is worth our while to spend a little time upon it.

First, it must be noticed that in all the writing's of Marx and Engels, whose "Anti-Duehring" always constitutes a necessary complement to all the theories of Marx, there is no proof of the asserted "necessity" of the social movement which fully satisfies the demands of our day as to scientific method. It is known that Marx stands upon the Hegelian dialectic, out of date now. What we demand is a psychological founding of social happening, and for this Marx cares little.

Now it seems to me easy to fill this gap. I shall attempt it so far as the limitations of time allow.

Why must the ideal of every proletarian movement be necessarily a democratic collectivism--that is, the communisation of the means of production? It seems to me that the following considerations contain the answer to the question.

The modern social movement strives after that which is represented by the battle-cry, "The emancipation of the proletariat." But this has two phases, an ideal and a material. Ideally a social class can consider itself as "emancipated" only when it as a class is economically and politically dominant or at least independent; the proletariat, that now finds itself in economic dependence upon capital, can only become "emancipated" by throwing off this connection. Perhaps we can conceive of the proletariat as using employers as agents to carry on the work of production. But even then the management will be no longer in the hands of the employers as to-day, but of the proletariat as master of the situation. So long as this supremacy is not reached in any such form, there can be no thought of an "emancipation" of a class. Nor can we speak of this "emancipation" in a material sense, so long as those conditions obtain which to-day, from a class standpoint, are looked upon as marking a social inferiority and are derived from the capitalistic social system. If the proletariat sets an aim clearly before itself, this goal can only be, from the class standpoint, the overthrow of this capitalistic order. Now this overthrow is possible in either of two ways. Either operations on a large scale, which have replaced the earlier and smaller methods of production, can be so reconstituted as that large interlocal and international production shall be again narrowed and localised--in which case the overthrow of the capitalistic order will be simply a retrogression to the "middle-class" system. Or this present order can be conquered in such a way that the existing forms of production on a large scale shall be retained--then the results will be socialism. There is no third possibility. If the proletariat does not vanquish capitalism by a return to the smaller forms of operation, it can accomplish this only by putting a socialistic organisation in place of the capitalistic. And further: the proletariat can attach itself only to the latter method, because its whole existence is interwoven with the system of production on a large scale; it is indeed only the shadow of the system, it exists only where this system rules. Therefore we can say that socialism as the aim of the social movement arises fundamentally and necessarily out of the economic situation of the proletariat. The whole demonstration falls to the ground in a moment, wherever a tendency to the development of proletarian production on a large scale does not exist in economic life.

What I would here show, let me say again, is the necessity of the ideal; but this must not be confused with the certainty of its realisation. In order to prove this, it would be necessary to present other considerations, which lie far from our subject. Thus, whether any such realisation of the ideal is scientifically possible seems to be doubtful. For this would not be proved even if it should be demonstrated that what the proletariat desires and strives for has been provided in the course of social development. I shall have opportunity later to draw attention to this, that the conception of socialism as a need of nature, and thus "necessarily" to be realised, does not rest upon clear thought.

What we must now hold fast as the result of our investigation is this, and it is a true Marxian thought, that social ideals are only utopianism so long as they are merely evolved in the head of the theorist. They obtain reality only when they are united to actual economic conditions, when they arise out of these conditions. The possibility of realising the good and beautiful is enclosed within the sheath of economic necessity. This covering, created out of capitalistic and proletarian conditions and historic economic circumstances, is of such a nature that the ideal of proletarian exertion can only lie in the direction of a socialistic order of society.

But why must the way towards the realisation of this aim lie through class strife? To this we answer in brief: modern society presents itself to us as an artificial medley of numerous social classes--that is, of certain groups of persons whose homogeneity arises out of their attachment to specific forms or spheres of economic life. We distinguish the "junker," as representative of feudal agrarianism, from the bourgeoisie, the representatives of capital; we distinguish the "middle class," the representatives of local production and distribution, from the modern wage-worker or the proletariat, etc. Each one of these groups of economic interests has its special adherents in the professional classes of society among the officials, scholars, artists, who stand outside the economic life, but who unite themselves by birth or position to one or another of the social classes.

This attachment to a social class works decisively in two directions. It implants in the mind of each individual member of a class the conception of the world and life characteristic of that group of men whose thoughts and feelings tend to become identical through the uniformity of the external circumstances that control them; similarity of aspiration and ideal is created. Further, this attachment accomplishes a positive control over the individual in the maintenance of that which is represented by the class--its social position as truly as its material interests; it creates what we may call class interest.

Everywhere and spontaneously there is developed a distinction between classes, and class interest is involved in this. The upholding of this class interest leads throughout to class opposition. Not always does the upholding of a class standard involve necessarily collision with the interests of other classes; at times an identity of interests arises; but this harmony never lasts. The interest of the "junker" must at a certain point come into conflict with that of the burgher, that of the capitalist with that of the proletariat, that of the hand-worker and tradesman with that of the large capitalist; for each class strives naturally for itself, and by that very fact excludes other interests. Then comes to pass the saying:

"Where one goes ahead, others go back; Who would not be driven must drive; So strife ensues and the strongest wins."

It is here that differences of opinion may emerge: but must this really come to "strife" and "warfare"? May we not hope that, through love of mankind, or sympathy, or interest in the welfare of the whole, or some such noble motive, each class will freely divest itself of such of its privileges as stand in the way of others? I have already had occasion in another place to express my opinion on this point--that I look upon such well-intentioned judgment of average human nature as in contradiction with actual life. I have referred to the fact that conclusive proof for or against such a conception cannot be presented; that the final ground of decision rests in the depths of personal conviction on the part of the individual. But what offers some proof for the justification of the realistic opinion presented by me is the circumstance that history has as yet given no example of a free divestment of class privilege; at least I will say that every instance claimed as such may easily be invalidated. On the other side we have innumerable instances in history where such reform has been begun by well-meaning friends of humanity, theorists, only to be shattered soon on the rocher de bronze of the strong self-interest of the threatened dominant class. They eagerly hold up before us unbelievers the night of the

4th of August, 1789, and they forget the hundred burning castles in France. They remind us of the Prussian agrarian reforms, and forget not only the French Revolution but also the Declaration of 1816. They remind us--but why add illustrations? Let such men prove authentically a single case in history in which a social class has against its own interests and out of altruistic motives made an essential concession. Certainly there have been conspicuous individuals who have done this; why not? We see this daily. But a whole class--never! If this is so, then the word of the great realist must be true, that "only strength conquers." So we find as the conclusion of our thought, first a difference of classes, then class interests, then class opposition, finally class strife. It is thus that Marx would have developed his theory of class strife, and easily, if he had chosen to proceed upon a psychological foundation.

As we now turn to this theory itself and its significance for the social movement we are obliged, I think, to concede that the entrance of Karl Marx was a decisive turning-point in this agitation, because through him it was based upon a fundamentally changed conception of history and humanity. This change is occasioned by the fact that, in place of an idealistic, or rather partisan, way of looking at things, a realistic vision obtains, and thus for the social movement the idea of "revolution" passes into the thought of "evolution." The spirit of the nineteenth century supplants the spirit of the preceding centuries. You remember how I sought to make clear to you the essence of this spirit in connection with the teachings of the utopists; if I may be allowed to refer to it again, it is that idealistic conception of man and life,[1] cherished now only by the scholars, that faith in humanity as good by nature, that belief that men so long as they are not led astray by the mistake or malice of individual bad men will live in the most affectionate peace with their brethren; it is that belief in a "natural order" of the past and future--that rock-fast confidence that only explanation and exhortation are needed in order to bring men out of this vale of tears to the happy islands of the blest. This is that faith in the power of eternal love which through its own force shall overcome the bad, and help the good to victory. This it was that, though the leaders were not conscious of it, really lay at the bottom of all political and social agitation until the middle of our century; this it is that, in my opinion, as I have already said, still slumbers in the lap of anarchism, even to-day as an instinct. This fundamental tendency is now directly reversed; the belief in a humanity good by nature gives place to the conviction that man is of himself ruled by no noble motives, that he carries within himself the bete humaine even in all culture and in spite of all "advance." Hence the conclusion: that a man, in order to accomplish anything in the world, must before all call upon "interest"--a normal and material instinct. For it is the most important conclusion for the fate of the social movement, that now "interest" rules in the world; that where anything is to be done, or a class, like the proletariat, is to be emancipated, a man needs some weapon stronger than the theory of "eternal love" against the interest of the capitalist class, and must present force against force, might armed by "interest." At the end of all thought upon this matter lies this consideration, which leads not only to the theory, but as well to the practice, of class strife. Combat is the solution of the difficulty for this hard and unlovely proletarian generation which has grown up since the middle of our century; not peace, not reconciliation, not a general brotherhood--but battle. That this strife is no longer open warfare, like street riot, does not alter the fact that it is really strife. Out of this is to come a generation of men qualified to live and work in an order of society higher than the present capitalistic order.

It is this that I call the realistic conception of the social movement; and there is no doubt that it is the outcome of that Marxian theory of the world and society which I have just attempted to sketch. Only thus could the social-political realism, which heretofore has been proclaimed in a limited way, now arise as the principle of the whole social movement.

It is this social-political realism which gives the finishing stroke to all utopism and revolutionism. The insurrectionists in Lyons and the Chartist revolutionaries were both utopists--for they shed their blood and yet only strengthened the reaction. The Putschists, Clubists, and Blanquists were utopists, who through conspiracies and street riots would through all time control economic development. Not less utopian were those "geniuses" who offered exchange banks or the Organisation du travail or such remedies.

Utopists also were those who believed in the power of all kinds of schemes. Finally, utopists were all those kindly souls who hoped to allay and overcome the sufferings of the proletariat by an appeal to the good hearts of the friends of humanity. Karl Marx has succeeded in freeing us from the use of empty phrases in the sphere of social politics.

Let us now in closing recapitulate the points wherein I see the historic significance of Marx's teaching for the social movement. Marx points out as its object the communisation of the means of production, as its way the struggle between classes; he erects these two as the main pillars upon which the whole structure must be built. He secured for these principles general acceptance; and he succeeded in this without preventing the development of national and other peculiarities. In placing the social movement in the flow of historic development he brings it theoretically into harmony with the objective and subjective factors of history, he bases it upon actual conditions of economic life and of human endowment, he shows its economic and psychological features.

Thus I look at Marx, when I attempt to fathom the spirit of his teaching; this is the deep meaning of Marxism.

There is no doubt that, according to the common idea, Marx and Engels, who must always be named with him, appear in a light essentially different from that which I have attempted to show to you. In general these men have been looked upon, not only as different from what I have stated, but as in a bad sense the very opposite of social realists; namely, as the father and the guardian of the worst kind of revolutionary thought. And who would not apparently be justified in this belief, reading the writings of both these men? He reads of clanking chains which must be broken, of revolutions towards which man tends, of bloody battle and death and assassination. How does the matter really lie?

Marx himself once said, Moi je ne suis pas Marxiste, but he gave to these words a meaning different from the ordinary one, as I also do when I say that

Marx and Engels have not always shown themselves consistent Marxists either in theory or in practice.

Doubtless there are inconsistencies in theory, contradictions of the fundamental thoughts, discrepancies which can have only one source--that is, an overwhelming revolutionary passion which obscures a vision otherwise so clear.

For example, I think of their unreasonable belief in what they call the "fall" of humanity through the introduction of the principle of private property, from which as they say history, and as well the forces of history, take their start; the astonished hearer asks himself, What impelled man to the introduction of this principle? I think, also, of the hypothesis of a strifeless condition of humanity after the introduction of socialism--and the like. Here, and throughout, the old dreams of a Paradise lost and regained, of a happy condition of humanity originally, come as a disturbing element into their new world of thought.

With both these men it was in life as in theory. Here also appears the old revolutionary Adam every moment and plays tricks with them. Since the year 1845 they have not ceased to dream of revolution, and indeed fierce revolution; repeatedly have they announced the outbreak as near. This could be only the outcome of an unrealistic judgment of the situation, of a mistaken conception of the political, economic, and social conditions; thus it was an error of judgment as to the time, if not a contradiction of their supreme principle that "revolutions are not made." Psychologically these contradictory phenomena are easily to be explained. Both Marx and Engels have never ceased with intelligence and calm judgment to present that realism which we have seen as the essence of their view of life. But you must not forget that they have conceived their teachings under the roar of revolutionary battles; that they were themselves of those fitful and fiery souls who, like the "world squirrel,"[2] go assiduously from place to place in order to set Europe on fire. Think of the mass of malice and hatred that must have accumulated within these exiles, who experienced through life nothing but derision, scorn, suspicion, and persecution from their powerful opponents! Imagine what a superhuman self-discipline and control was needed to prevent them from petty and vindictive attacks upon the hated opponents at every opportunity. As this deeply rooted passion arose in these revolutionary heroes, as rage almost strangled them, their logic flew out of the window and old revolutionary fury broke out and overwhelmed them. But that I am right in characterising Marxism as a social-political realism you see clearly from the many and fundamental declarations and acknowledgments of its founders, which come to us out of all periods of their lives. And indeed there is always a declared opposition to general revolutionism, to "Putschism," as they assert their standpoint. The strife with the party of Willich-Schapper in the year 1850, the battle with Bakunin in the "International,"--concerning which I have yet to speak,--the declarations against the anarchists, the discussion with Duehring, the disowning of the "Jungen,"--all tends in the end to help to victory the evolutionary principle in the social movement. It is easy to explain how the true conviction came to expression on these occasions.

The last word of Marxism, which also contains a resume of its teaching; is a writing by Engels, published shortly before his death; the introduction to the Struggle of Classes in France. It is an epilogue to his own life's drama, a confession, the last words of warning which the dying man cries to the contesting proletariat. Here the clear, logical position, as I think it is demanded by the conception of history held by that school, finally comes to distinct expression. This introduction shows perhaps best and most quickly how at the end Engels and Marx understood the social movement. Some of the most significant passages may here find place:

"History has proved wrong us and all who thought similarly (sc. expecting the victory of the proletariat in the near future of the year 1843). It has made clear that the condition of economic development upon the Continent at that time was far from ripe for an abolishment of capitalistic production; it has proved this through the economic development which since 1848 has seized upon the whole continent and has made a home for the great industries in France, Austria, Hungary, Poland, and lately Russia, has made out of Germany an industrial country of the first rank--all upon a capitalistic basis, which in the year 1848 was but little developed. To-day the great international army of socialists is resistlessly stepping forward, is daily growing in number, discipline, intelligence, and assurance of victory. As to-day this mighty army of the proletariat has not as yet reached the goal, as it is far from accomplishing the victory by one great stroke, but must slowly press forward in hard persistent struggle from position to position, this proves once for all how impossible it was in the year 1848 to accomplish the social overturning through a simple unexpected attack.... The time of surprise, of carrying through a revolution by a small minority at the head of ignorant masses, is passed. For a complete overthrow of the social organisation the masses themselves must be concerned, they must understand what they do, why they take part. The history of the last fifty years has taught this to us. But through this teaching the masses are learning what is to be done, and that long and patient work is needed, and that it is just this work which we now urge forward with such success that our opponents are brought to confusion. The irony of history turns everything upside down. We, 'revolutionaries,' succeed far better by means legal than illegal and destructive. The party of order, as it calls itself, goes to pieces through the very conditions created by itself. It cries out confusedly with Odelon Barrot--la legalite nous tue (conformity to the law kills us); while we, with this legality, develop round muscles and red cheeks and seem destined for eternal life."

What comes to expression in these words is merely a confession of--Marxism.

* * * * *

FOOTNOTES:

[1] In what follows I reproduce some passages out of my book concerning Friedrich Engels (Berlin, 1895).

[2] In German mythology the world is represented as a great tree, with its

roots in Niefelheim, and its branches in Asgard. Wotan communicates with the world by a "welten eichhoernchen," a "world squirrel," which runs up and down the tree. (Translator.)

CHAPTER VI

THE TREND TOWARDS UNITY

"Schon laengst verbreit etsich's in ganze Scharen Das Eigenste, was im allein gehoert."

SCHILLER's Wallenstein.

Now, after long, that diffuses itself through large masses of men Which once was most private, which belonged to him alone.

Karl Marx closed his manifesto with the celebrated words, "Proletarians of all lands, unite yourselves!" He uttered this cry on the eve of the revolution of 1848, which was admittedly proletarian-socialistic in its character, in various places, but which exhausted itself in those separate spots where it had broken out. In Germany, where Marx himself stood in the battle, it reached no importance. In England, it seemed for a moment as if the February revolution would infuse new life into the old Chartism; but this had already been buried. The French movement is the only one left; how it ended is well known. And then the deep night of the reaction of the 'fifties settled upon Europe. All the seeds of an independent working-men's movement were suppressed. Only in England the trade-union movement was developed.

Since the beginning of the year 1860 signs of life among the working people have appeared in different places. They recover here and there from the blows and repression which they experienced during and after the agitation of 1848, and an interest and participation in public life begin again to awake. The characteristic trait is this: the activity of the new and independent life receives an international stamp. Naturally this is no mere chance. It was not by chance that, at the World's Exposition, the working men of different lands first reached the hand one to another; it was a development of capitalism itself, stepping upon a stage of international largeness. The Continental powers of Europe began to rival England. Commercial politics were first of all robbed of their exclusive character through a series of treaties, and were directed towards the unifying of business life throughout Europe.

Since those first beginnings, at about the year 1860, the idea of internationalism has never quite disappeared from proletarian agitation, even though it may have experienced in the course of the years essential changes in the form of its development.

It will be my duty in what follows to show to you how this tendency towards internationalism, after many abortive attempts, has been really carried out, and how, in close connection with it as concerns goal and progress, the social agitations of individual lands more and more press towards a unity upon the principles of the Marxian programme.

The first form in which an attempt was made for international combination of the proletariat is the celebrated "International." Allow me to dwell somewhat at length upon this. It is essentially of importance and interest for two reasons. One is that through it, and its speedy end, a specific form of the internationalising of the social agitation has been brought ad absurdum. The other is because in it with striking clearness contradictions are presented, which pervade all social agitation.

It was in the year 1862, when the French working-men, at the World's Exposition in London, agreed with the English workers to counsel together concerning united agitation. Further conferences ensued, and in 1864 a union was founded which had as its object the uniting of the representatives of workmen of different lands for common action and advance. This was the International Association. What were the duties, what was the thought, of such a brotherhood? Apparently twofold. We can suppose that they meant to create merely a kind of correspondence bureau--a place where the working men of different lands might unite in a general international secretariate, to which they might turn for information concerning any question pertaining to the social movement--that is, an institution far from exerting an influence upon the agitations of the working men in the various lands. The majority of the men who, at that time, in the beginning of the 'sixties, strove to carry out the idea of an international union thought of it surely in this vague form.

The other conception goes further; a central spot should be created for the working-men's movement, a place from which the working-men's agitations in turn might receive assistance and inspiration, from which influence could be exerted upon the separate national efforts. The most important representative of the latter and larger meaning was Karl Marx, who was called upon to play a decisive role in the founding of the International Working-Men's Association. For him this organisation was the first answer to his cry to the world, "Proletarians of all lands, unite yourselves!" It is not to be doubted that if a central organisation was to be created, to reveal a spirit of unity and to ensure a unification of national proletarian agitation, the Marxian spirit should control. Although he viewed the situation clearly enough to see that extremest caution was needed, he aimed to unite the many streams into one great river.

The "International" was founded upon the basis of the so-called "Inaugural Address" and the "Statutes," both of which were evolved by Karl Marx and accepted as he presented them. In them great diplomatic skill is revealed. The "Inaugural Address" is a masterpiece of diplomatic finesse. It is indefinite throughout its whole structure, rendered purposely so by Karl Marx. He aimed, by it, to cover various parties of the time, the Proudhonists, the working-men's associations of France, the trade unions in England, the followers of Mazzini in Italy, the supporters of the Lassalle agitation in Germany; and it actually accomplished this in a masterly way. It commended itself to each and every one of them. It pictures in effective way the misery into which the working people are plunged by capitalism; it finds words of recognition for the results of the English trade unions. It praises the characteristics and services of the "free-cooperative movement"--Proudhon,

Duchez; but it has also a friendly word for the organisations which receive aid from the state--Lassalle, Blanc.

Out of it all is drawn only this conclusion, with which all sympathise--that the proletariat of all lands should be conscious of an international solidarity. In some general and sentimental phrases, which surely were traced by Marx with reluctance, national differences find their adjustment, and their representatives find a uniting bond. The "Statutes" were prefaced by some considerations which contained in nuce the principles of Marxism--with various concessions, as, for example, the appeal to verite, justice et morale. But even here is all pressure avoided. A man could, on any point of uncertainty, always think that something else was meant, and could at least feel himself free concerning it. Very little reference was made to the objects of the International Working-Men's Association. Its activity during the first years consisted essentially in the support of strikes, for which reason it enjoyed at the beginning the lively sympathy of many outside of the circles of working men.

But now Marx began to develop his plan systematically; that is, slowly to fill the International Working-Men's Association with his spirit, and through it to support the proletarian agitation of different lands. As we look at the congresses of this organisation, in Geneva, 1866; Lausanne, 1867; Brussels, 1868; Basle, 1869, we find that in fact, step by step, from congress to congress, the International Working-Men's Association supports more and more the Marxian ideas, noticeably, and without any appearance of the moving spirit on the scene. But now it is interesting to observe, and it shows the degree of development which at that time the social movement had reached, that the time for the inspiration of the whole European world of working men with the Marxian ideas evidently had not yet come. In proportion as the "International" began to display the spirit of Marx, opposition raged in every quarter. The Proudhonists began to oppose it; then the trade unions, especially after that moment when Marx declared himself in sympathy with the Commune in Paris; the followers of Lassalle began to grumble at it. A great part of the opposition crystallised itself, towards the end of the 'sixties, in one man, Michael Bakunin. As to the part which personal anger and envy played in this opposition, we are not interested. It is possible that this personal friction was essentially the reason for the destruction of the "International." It seems to me, however, that at the bottom of the antagonism of Bakunin against Marx lay a much more essential and considerable opposition. For in 1868 Bakunin founded the Alliance Internationale de la Democratie Sociale, in which he united chiefly Italian and Spanish associations, and as well the French; and it is in this alliance that the opposition on principle to Marx's efforts comes to clear and sharp expression. But the real point of difference lies in the distinction which you already know between revolutionism on the one side and the evolution idea on the other, between the idealistic and the realistic conception of history. Bakunin based his whole activity upon the idea of revolution by force, upon the belief that revolutions must be made because they can be made. In opposition to him, Marx defended the fundamental thought that a revolution is at most the last feature of a process of development, the breaking of the husk through the ripening of the fruit.

The opposition of Bakunin led finally, as is well known, to the dissolution of the International Working-Men's Association. In 1872 its general office was transferred to New York, apparently in order to avoid a formal burial of the organisation.

Thus it came to pass that the Bakunists were shut out, and with them were a number of "exclusions" from the circles of the orthodox; the process of excommunication began, which to-day, as you know, is not ended. Exactly the same thought lies at the bottom of the exclusion of the Bakunists from the "International" as, this very year, in the driving of the anarchists out of the London congress. Always again the contradiction presents itself, socialism and anarchism; or, as deeply understood, evolutionism and revolutionism.

Thus was shattered that first attempt to make a union of the proletariat of all lands, and it will be many years before the thought of international solidarity can again rule the working man. In spite of its speedy ruin, the

"International" has large historic significance, and this lies in the fact that for the first time it brought the internationalism of the movement and the international community of interest of the proletariat in some measure to clear expression; further, in that for the first time the social movement of different lands was made familiar with the Marxian scheme of thought, and at the same time affected with the Marxian spirit.

The compromises of the Marxian scheme gave the first impulse to the general linking of international social agitation. But finally this unification would be accomplished in a way quite other than that which the founder of the International Working-Men's Association had imagined. A mistake as to way was made; for this reason the "International" went down. It had placed before itself the task of forcing solidarity into the social movement from without, inwards. This is a thought which is essentially un-Marxian; again, one of the cases in which Marx was not Marxian. The way to unity should have been reversed; from within, outwardly. First must the agitations in individual lands be divested to some degree of their national and contingent features, first must the general economic development be further advanced, before the proletariat could by internal development become conscious of its international solidarity and come to a recognition of this unity in the chief points of its programme.

This internal and external unification, which is the product of the last decade, I might specify as the third stage in the development of the social movement; and then the second stage would be the complete saturation of the German social democracy with the Marxian spirit. This political party becomes thereby the organ through which those ideas spread into other lands.

In Germany there has grown into recognition a social movement which, at the beginning, was conducted in the spirit of both Marx and Lassalle, but which soon came under the control of pure Marxism. I recall the following stages of development. When thirty-two years ago the deadly bullet struck Lassalle in Geneva, that man was removed who alone had represented the German working-men's movement; and what he left behind was next to nothing. His "Working-Men's Union" numbered only four thousand six hundred and ten members at the moment when he closed his eyes. So also immediately after Lassalle's death the agitation was nothing more than a useless and petty strife. It was a coterie rather than a social party. Thus the field in Germany was open for the development of a new social-democratic movement from another source. This was started in 1864 by Wilhelm Liebknecht, who came to Germany as the direct envoy of Karl Marx, and with strong belief in his ideas; the purpose was to establish the working-men's movement upon a basis other than that of Lassalle. He won to this cause the youthful energy of the master-turner August Bebel, who, at the age of twenty-four, was already the leader of a number of working-men's unions which had been until that time in advanced radicalism. These are the organisations, you know, which in the year 1868, in Nuremberg, seceded from Schulze to Marx. Fourteen thousand working men were represented. The resolution through which this transfer was accomplished was drawn by Liebknecht and was inspired by the Marxian spirit. Thus in 1868 a new social party was formed in Germany which took the name of the Social-Democratic Working-Men's Party, and which, after the congress in Eisenach, stood for a time alone as the so-called "Honorables," until in the year 1875 the union of the Lassalle and the Bebel faction was accomplished in Gotha. Since that time, as you know, the one "Social-Democratic Party" exists. It is significant that the present union rests upon a compromise between Lassalle and Marx, but is really directed by the Marxists, who step by step have won control in the party. The "Gotha" programme remained as the platform of the movement in Germany for sixteen years; and not until the year 1891 was it replaced by a new platform, the "Erfurt" programme, which now constitutes the confession of faith of the Social-Democratic movement in Germany. It is pervaded by a strongly Marxian spirit and contains essentially only a statement of Marxian doctrines in accordance with the spirit of the age. Let me in a few words present merely the lines of thought in this programme. It begins with the phrases:

"The economic development of middle-class society leads by a necessity of nature to the extinction of that economic order, production on a small scale, which rests upon the private ownership of the workman in his means of production. It separates the workman from his means of production, and changes him into a possessionless proletarian; while the instruments of production become the monopoly of a small number of capitalists and landowners, etc."

As you see, this programme proceeds from the fundamental thought that economic development completes itself in a specific way; hence follow all the other matters with which the programme deals. This special Marxian thought, that an economic evolution is involved, has become the central point of the Erfurt programme. It shows, further, how out of the economic development a conflict emerges in the form of class strife; and then it concludes that only a change to communal ownership of the means of production can quiet this conflict. The party for which the platform was created takes hold of the communistic thought of the Erfurt programme in this sense, that the duty of a political party can only be to bring to the consciousness of the workman the existing economic revolution.

These are the words: "To bring this warfare of the working classes to consciousness and unity, to show the natural and necessary goal--that is the duty of the Social-Democratic Party." This is the point that is especially important for us--the German agitation becomes completely saturated, rapidly and uninterruptedly, with Marxian ideas, and thus this spirit spreads gradually into other lands.

If you now ask me how this gradual extension of the Marxian system and in connection with it the unification of the Marxian movement are shown, the following, points seem to me of especial importance. In 1873 the "International" came to an end. It seemed as if, with it, the internationalisation of the social movement in like manner had ceased. But for about a decade past we have had again general and formal "International Working-Men's Congresses." The year 1889 opened the series with a working-men's congress in Paris, again at a world's exposition. Here again, in a new and freer form, this idea of the old "International" arises, and in a much larger form than the old international working-men's associations had ever realised it. For these former international working-men's associations had been really only a combination of a number of representatives and secretaries. The masses scarcely stood upon paper. The congresses which now again the world of working men have created rest upon a much broader basis, in my opinion, since, in spite of all "exclusions" and factional strife, these international meetings represent a real combination of working men conscious of their aim and organised for it--a fact which we can no longer hide from ourselves, since the old English trade-unions have become represented at the congresses. Thus the international congresses now include the so-called "socialists" and the trade unions as well. In spite of all differences of opinion on certain points, at these congresses there is such expression of internationality and solidarity on the part of the proletariat as was never approached by any of the meetings of the old "International." And it is certainly not by chance that the pictures of Marx and Engels look down upon these new unions of the international proletariat.

But let us now look at a number of evidences, which make clear to us that the movements of different lands approach more and more to a unanimity resting upon the leading thoughts of the Marxian programme. There is first the important fact to remember that the French, originally uneconomic in temperament, have now begun effectively the trade-union agitation. The creation of Bourses du Travail prove how earnestly this part of the social movement is cultivated by the French. Through the agitation of class strife, the general movement towards such associations receives a new impulse. And as the French, inclined to revolutionary and political agitation, begin to become economic, we see on the other side the very important fact that the English working-man recedes step by step from his purely trade-union "Manchester" platform.

I have never believed what some years ago was announced to the world, in connection with a snap resolution of a working-men's congress, that the English trade-unions would go over to the socialistic camp with torch and trumpet. Such decisive changes in social life are not accomplished in that way;

there is needed a slow ripening. And the proceedings of the London congress in this year (1896) prove how much antipathy yet exists between the English trade-unions and certain elements of Continental socialism. But in spite of all these tendencies the fact remains that the English working-men's movement approaches the Continental on important points; that is, it has at least begun to be socialistic in aim and political in the means used. That an "Independent Working-Men's Party" as yet plays no role in England proves for the present nothing. The peculiar conditions of English party life make a representation of the working men in Parliament unnecessary under the circumstances. But who can doubt, in view of the proceedings of the last decade, that the English trade-unions, even the older ones, stretch out the hand more than formerly towards the door-latch of legislation? Let me remind you of the fact that with small, though deeply interested, minorities the trade unions have written upon their programme a legal work-day of eight hours. Also, in spite of much limitation and qualification, the resolution of the English working-men in the year 1894 remains--the communisation of the English means of production, at least the most important of them, as the object of their agitation. Is that anything other than a conversion of the English working-men's association?

In Germany we find that the normal line, upon which the social movement in all nations begins to arrange itself, was nearly reached at the start. It was only necessary to throw off some of Lassalle's peculiar ideas, those revolutionary notions which arose here and there about the year 1870, and especially to give broader play to the trade-union movement, in order to reach the "minimum programme" of all social agitation. This programme is, to repeat concisely:--the object of the social movement is the communisation of the means of production in its largest technical development upon a democratic basis; the means of reaching this aim is the struggle of classes; this has two equally justifiable forms, the economic--which finds its expression in the trade-union movement, the political--which finds its expression in representation in Parliament. The formulation of this proposition is the specific service of Karl Marx, as we have seen; and for this reason I think I am warranted in speaking of the whole social movement of our time as infused with the Marxian spirit. For it is not unknown to you that the social agitation in lands of later capitalistic development--Italy, Austria, and Russia--has been from the beginning in accordance with the thought of that platform.

If in any such way I think that I see a unification of the social movement, that does not mean that I see a machine-like uniformity of this movement in the different lands. I am not blind to the innumerable diversities which are developed by the various nations, and which are revealed every moment. I have attempted to show to you how absolutely necessary these national peculiarities are, and to a certain degree always will be--because of historic tradition and difference of national character. So when I speak of a unity, I only mean, as I have already often said, a tendency to this which struggles to assert itself in spite of national disposition. The social agitation will always retain a double tendency, a centripetal and a centrifugal. The former, arising from the uniformity of capitalistic development and from the similarity of original causes, tends towards conformity; the latter, the product of national differences and of manifold causes, tends to divergence.

I have to-day attempted to show to you how the centripetal tendency reveals itself. The object of my next lecture will be to present to you a systematic review of the manifold points of difference which have already often been referred to in the course of these lectures. Thus will be completed the picture of the essentials of the modern social movement, which I am attempting to sketch for you.

CHAPTER VII

TENDENCIES OF THE PRESENT

"Usually a man refuses to dismiss the fool that he carries within, and to admit any great mistake, or to acknowledge any truth that brings him to despair."

GOETHE, Wilhelm Meister's Apprenticeship.

Who, caring at all about what is going on in these days, has not noticed the many contradictions which are now apparent in the great social movement? Even the inexperienced observer, or he who stands too near to real life to have free and wide outlook, will easily see behind these contradictions a tendency towards a unity of effort. Now that we have obtained a right understanding of this we shall, I hope, do justice to these differences, these contradictions--we shall be able to comprehend them in their essence and necessity.

The sources out of which they spring are as numerous as the contradictions themselves. How often a personal motive can, under certain circumstances, appear as an essential difference! Morbid self-conceit, desire for power, quarrelsomeness, caprice, malevolence, lack of honour--innumerable traits of character give occasion for friction and contention.

But for these the social theorist cares nothing. Only that is of importance to him which rests upon an essential difference. And of these also there are enough, because the causes of them are numerous. What is here decisive is the variation in the view of world and life, is the difference of national character, is the varying degree of vision into the essence of social development or of understanding concerning accepted principles, is the varying measure of ripeness and education of the masses, is the difference in economic development in the various lands, etc.

But I cannot possibly exhaust the points of contradiction and strife which arise out of these manifold and effective causes. I shall here simply present certain matters which seem to me especially important because essentially significant. My duty as to this problem can be, again, only that of a theorist who tries to make a clear explanation, who desires not to work upon your will but upon your intelligence, who does not carry in his hand the brand of agitation but the lamp of illumination.

If I do not pay attention to some points of difference which may seem to you of supreme importance, it is not because I do not myself recognise this importance, but because I suppose the contradiction that comes to expression in them to be either out of date or only imaginary, or because I go back of them to the deeper, essential differences. Thus, for example, the alternative, trade unions or a working-men's party, is either the expression of a deeper opposition concerning which I shall later speak, or it is a question that does not concern us in these days. Thus concerning all those representatives of the working-men's movement who place themselves upon the platform of legal struggle. These men know that politics and trade unions are like the right and left legs upon which the proletariat marches; that political part-taking is needed in order to obtain influence upon legislation; that economic organisation is needed in order to discipline and educate the masses. The only question can be now as to the degree, the more or less, of the one or the other form of social agitation;--always within the limits of legal agitation on the part of the working men. Any such question cannot be general; it must be decided separately in each place and case. The economic ripeness of the masses, the degree of political freedom, and much else, must decide.

In a similar way is another point of difference to be judged; shall there be an independent working-men's party or not? You know, I have already spoken to you a number of times concerning this, saying that in England thus far there has been practically no independent working-men's party; I have given to you the reasons why, as it seems to me, any such party has been until now at least unnecessary, even if the working men desired to busy themselves in political matters. The political influence of the social movement is not dependent upon the existence of an independent party of working men. Even that question is not a general one; it must be decided according to local circumstances.

If we ask now for antitheses of real importance, we are met first and especially, to-day, by that sufficiently explained opposition which is contained in the words revolution or evolution, the old point of discussion which was, is, and I believe will be, a constant feature of social agitation; that point of separation which we traced first in the "International," and which to-day we see revived in the opposition of the so-called "Junger" and the anarchists against the majority of organised labour. The reasons on account of which I think that also in the future this discussion will not cease are as follows. Revolutionism is, as I have shown you, a manifestation of unripeness. A man can, in a certain sense, assert that the social movement begins anew every moment; for every day new masses arise out of the lower strata of the proletariat yet living in stupid unconsciousness, and they attach themselves to the social movement. These unschooled elements, of course, in their part-taking show the characteristics of the social movement itself in its beginnings. They find their natural leaders in the disinherited citizens of the day, like Catiline of old, mostly young men who have nothing to lose and who try to substitute a fiery enthusiasm for theoretic insight and practical judgment. The process which we have watched for a decade is one which must ever again be repeated; the maturer elements are absorbed and disappear, new hordes of revolutionists arise, and the process of absorption by the riper, evolutionary, elements begins anew. Thus we see two opposing phases of the development of social agitation that play their part at the same time in different spheres of the proletariat. So far as can be seen, there has been thus far an uninterrupted progress in the absorption of the unripe revolutionary elements by the evolutionists.

But even here, where the idea of evolution, consciously or unconsciously, obtains recognition as the basis of the social movement, we meet questions, many of which, as it seems to me, arise because of a false conception of the essence of social evolution.

Although I have had opportunity at different times to show what social evolution is, at least in a general way, let me here repeat concisely what I understand by this idea; for a right comprehension of this point is all-important. Social evolution, and the conception of the social movement as such an evolution, rest upon the thought that we find ourselves in a continued condition of economic and thus social change, and that specific social interests and the necessary relations of mastery are connected with each change; thus in proportion as the evolution proceeds and as the activities of the interested groups develop, the balance of power becomes displaced, with the result that the ruling classes are slowly replaced by other classes that reach control. Here also lies at bottom the thought that the division of power at any given time is truly the expression of economic relations, and is no merely accidental and artificial work; that this power can only be displaced gradually, and only as the economic relations are changed, and as at the same time the personal and subjective conditions and the characteristics of the aspiring classes are developed. In a word, social evolution is a gradual achievement of power, the creation of a new condition of society, corresponding to the overthrow of economic relations and the transformation and schooling of character.

Among the evolutionists differences have emerged owing to a confusion of the terms "quietism" and "evolution." Especially among the Marxists has the thought spread, that evolution is so entirely a process of nature, independent of human activity, that the individual must let his hands rest in his lap and must wait until the ripened fruit drops. This quietist and, as I believe, pseudo-Marxist idea has no real connection with the inner thought of evolution. Its fundamental mistake lies in the fact that all the occurrences in social life are carried out by living men, and that men complete the process of development by placing aims before themselves and by striving to realise these aims.

The standpoints of the social theorist and of him who deals practically in social life are entirely different; but men constantly interchange the two. For the theorist, social development is a necessary sequence of cause and effect, as he sees it in the shaping of life compulsorily by the motives of the persons involved; and these motives themselves he tries to understand in their limitations. For him social life is a process rather of the past. But for the man who deals practically in social life, it lies in the future. What the theorist understands as the working of specified causes is, to the practical man, an object lying in the future which his will should help to accomplish. This very will is a necessary element in the causation of social happening. And this will, conditioned as it may be, is the highest personal possession of man in action. As the social theorist seeks to show as necessary specific tendencies of the will, and with them specific developments of the social life, he can do this with the self-evident limitation that the energy of the practical man in creating and accomplishing these efforts of the will does not fail. If for any reason, for example through the pressure of quietistic sentiment, this energy should be lessened, the most important link in the assumed chain of causes would drop out, and the development would take an entirely different course. It is a great mistake to apply unqualifiedly to social life the idea of a process in accordance with natural law; for example, to say that socialism must come by a "necessity of nature." Socialism has nothing to do with any such necessity. Thus, for example, we cannot see why the development of capitalism should not lead just as well to the overthrow of modern culture. And it must surely take this course if the leaders of advance do not develop during the transformation of the social life the necessary qualities for a new order of society, if they allow themselves to sink into a marasmus or quietism. For them, all social happening is only a condition to be created: and in order to accomplish this in the future they need an energy of resolution.

In close connection with the point of which we have just spoken stands another matter, which also in the last analysis depends upon a right understanding of the essence of social evolution. I refer to the confusion of "ideal" and "programme"--the substitution of politics for idealism. I mean this: superficial evolutionists, especially in the ranks of the Marxists, are inclined to look with supreme contempt upon idealists and enthusiasts, and to rest only upon practical politics; they emphasise the rational to the exclusion of the ideal. That is a conception which does not at all harmonise with the real meaning of evolution. For evolution wants its highest social ideals to be realised, but these are founded only upon postulates essentially ethical. To realise these ideals it is necessary to become inspired, to kindle a heart's glow, to develop a fire of enthusiasm. The warming sun must shed its beams, if all is not to go under and become darkened--with danger of the annihilation of all life. The word of the dying St. Simon, with which he took departure from his favourite scholar Rodriguez, is eternally true: "Never forget, my friend, that a man must have enthusiasm in order to accomplish great things." When this idealism and enthusiasm disappear from a movement, when its impetus is lost, when it passes into a littleness of opportunism, into an emptiness of small politics, it dies like a body without life. And it is certainly one of the most unpleasant traits of many of the modern representatives of the proletarian movement, that in the dusty atmosphere of common politics they have lost their enthusiasm and have sunk to the level of political malcontents.

But on the other side, we must not confuse idealism with fantasy or utopism. Enthusiasm for an object should be combined with common sense. In the one is warmth, in the other clearness; in the one lies the ideal, in the other the programme, that will offer ways and means for reaching the end.

Only when we learn to distinguish between these two fundamental thoughts shall we be able to unite ideal enthusiasm with practical common sense. For as the confusion of programme with ideal tends on the one side to a decline into useless commonplace, so on the other side it leads to a crippling of practical activity. But he who learns to distinguish the road from the goal will see that tireless exertion is needed in order to press towards the mark. An understanding of the importance and necessity of gradual reform is only awakened as a deeper insight into the worth and essence of the ideal is obtained.

It must be allowed that a certain contradiction will remain in any full understanding of the evolution idea in a social movement. We cannot avoid the fact that the sceptical pessimist stands by the side of the light-hearted optimist; that there will always be some who hope for a speedy entrance into the promised land, while others are of the opinion that the march thereto lies through the wilderness and will last long. Hence the differences of position that men take regarding what we call practical reforms. Men who believe that we are about to move into a new building will not be willing to try to improve the old structure; but those who think that the new edifice may be long in rising will be contented to live for a while longer as comfortably as possible in the old structure. This contradiction is in the nature of man. It will continue ineradicable. It is enough for a man to be conscious of its existence.

What we have learned to recognise thus far of antithesis rests upon essentially different conceptions of the essence of social development or upon different interpretations of one of these conceptions--the evolutionary. Let me now, in a few words, speak of a matter which rests upon the different interpretations--at least when they arise to consciousness--which men place upon the progress and the direction of social development. This contradiction rests upon a variation of ideal, and consequently of programme; and it may be expressed in the antithesis democratic or socialistic. In order to understand properly this most important contradiction, which to-day stands as the central point of discussion and which finds its acutest expression in the exciting "agrarian question," I must remind you of something said heretofore--at that hour when I spoke to you concerning the necessary limitation of the proletarian-socialistic ideal. You remember that there I specified as a necessary condition for the development of socialism as the object of the modern social movement, the previous development of capitalism and with it the impoverishment of the masses. There must be a thorough proletarian condition.

But now consider the following. When the proletariat sets up this object upon the basis of its economic conditions of existence, how will the proletariat conduct itself with all those strata of society who have not this same basis of economic existence? What will be the relation of the proletariat to those masses who are not yet made proletarian in character--as, for example, the lower middle-classes? And there is a question yet more important--What will be the relation of the proletariat to that part of the people, the demos, who cannot possibly ever have a tendency towards becoming proletarian? Here arises the great dilemma, and this is the deep contradiction which comes here to expression: Shall the aim of the proletariat remain essentially and preponderantly proletarian, or shall it become on the whole democratic? And further, if the working-men's party will interest itself in all these component parts of the demos, how shall the proletariat conduct itself with them? If there is to be a general democratic "people's party," what then becomes of the proletarian programme? For this is clear: the whole reason for the existence of socialistic agitation, as it is to-day attempted, with the cry of a "need of nature" in the economic development, falls to the ground in the moment when this economic development does not lead to the proletarianisation of the masses and to the communisation of the processes of production--to mercantile operations on a large scale. If socialism is postulated upon any other grounds of ethics or expediency, it cannot be "scientific" in the thought of the day. Here, as I believe, lies the justification for the antithesis "socialistic or democratic." And in the opposition of these two general thoughts, each of which is represented within the social movement, is expressed that deeply lying conflict of which we speak.

How these tendencies will settle themselves we cannot yet clearly see.

I believe that the following considerations may tend towards a clearing of the situation.

The whole strength of the social movement, all chances for the final victory of its ideas, so far as I see, rest upon the fact that it proposes to be the representative of the highest form of economic life at every period of production upon the largest scale. It tries to climb upon the shoulders of the bourgeoisie, who are now the representatives of the most highly developed forms of economy; and it thinks that it will be able to overtop. History teaches us that what we call advance has always been only change to a higher system of economy, and that those classes thrive who represent this higher system. Behind capitalism there is no "development"; possibly there may be ahead. The degree of production which has been reached by it must in any case be rivalled by any party that will secure the future for itself. In that is shown, I think, the standard of any advance movement.

If the social democracy is to maintain its historic mission, if it is to be a party of advance, it must avoid compromise with the notoriously declining classes, as the hand-workers and other economically low organisations. Even a temporary compact with them is dangerous. It will not be admissible, also, to change the programme and goal of the social movement to suit the middle-class elements that have crept in, if that great aim of production upon the largest scale shall be held fast--because we know positively that their hand-work represents in general a low form of economy. But now the other side of the question. If there are spheres in economic life which are not to be subjected to this process of communisation, because the smaller method of business is under the conditions more profitable than the larger,--how about the farmer? That is the whole problem which to-day stands before the social democracy as the "agrarian question." Must the communistic ideal of production on a large scale, and the developed programme connected with it, undergo any essential change as applied to the peasantry? And if a man reaches the conclusion that in agrarian development no tendency to production on a large scale exists, but that here operation on a large scale is not at all the highest form of management, then we see before us the decisive question--Shall we now be democratic in the sense of allowing production on a small scale in this sphere and thus change our programme and desert the communistic ideal; or shall we remain proletarian, hold fast to the communistic ideal and exclude this class from our movement? In this case the former decision would not be reactionary, because, in spite of the acceptance of that lower middle-class element into the movement, it is not necessary to come down from the level of production that has been reached in the spheres of industry that have been communised.

I have here been obliged to speak doubtfully because thus far, so far as I know, there is no certainty either as to the tendency of development among the agriculturalists or as to the form of management, nor are we certain as to whether any specific form of agrarian production is the superior. But, so far as I see, the Marxian system breaks down on this point; the deductions of Marx are not applicable to the sphere of agriculture without change. He has said much of importance concerning agrarian matters; but his theory of development, which rests upon an assumption of business upon a large scale and upon the proletarianising of the masses, and which necessarily leads to socialism in its development, is only for the sphere of manufactures. It does not apply to agricultural development; and to me it seems that only a scientific investigation will be able to fill the gap which now exists.

Of far-reaching importance, and at this moment of pressing interest, are two points which I would present in conclusion. I mean the attitude of the social movement towards religion and towards nationality. Because here personal feeling and temperament may easily interfere with the clear vision of the observer, it is doubly necessary to divest oneself of all passion and to deal with these problems objectively. Let us make the attempt. Leaving out of consideration the English working-man, who to-day, as a generation ago, seems to oscillate between pietism and positivism, and who on this point cannot be considered typical because of the well-known peculiar conditions of his development, the proletarian movement doubtless is strongly anti-religious. How comes this?

So far as I see, the opposition to religion comes from two different sources: it has a "theoretical" and a "practical" origin. Theoretically the proletariat and its leaders have become heirs of the liberal "age of illumination." Out of a superficial study of natural sciences have sprung all these anti-religious writings of the years 1860-1880 which in an intoxication of joy announced the first recognition of the atheistic dogma to the world. These writers never rose above the level of "itinerant preachers of materialism," and they have never reached to the level of the Marx-Engels conception of life. The platform of this dogmatic atheism may be considered to-day as entirely something of the past. There is no earnest representative of science anywhere who to-day dares to assert that science means atheism and excludes religion. Thus the attitude of the proletariat towards religion would be entirely free and independent if the ground of its irreligion were merely a theoretic and misleading incursion into the dogmatism of natural science. But the enmity to religion has much deeper grounds. Not only has an enthusiasm for scientific materialism taken hold of the proletariat with special force; but also the enthusiasm for unbelief has been helped greatly in its development by the instinctive feeling, or the clear consciousness, that in the materialistic conception of the world lies the germ of a mighty revolutionary force, well suited to drive authority from all spheres of life. What wonder that the proletariat took hold of it as a useful weapon for the strife; for, as we know, one of the conditions of the very existence of the proletariat lies in a tearing asunder of all the old points of faith. Thus the predilection for materialism and atheism is well explained.

And now consider that the acceptance of this dogma betokens a protest against the Christian system of thought, which the working man must look upon as inimical because represented by the ruling classes and used in their interests. For there can be no doubt that, in an overwhelming majority of cases, official Christianity has been used by the ruling classes against the movement for the emancipation of the proletariat. The fate that falls upon heretical Christians is the best proof of this. So long as men try to support monarchy and capitalism as a necessary and Divine institution, using the Christian Church for this purpose, the social movement must become anti-ecclesiastical and thus anti-religious. Thus a mistrust as to the position, in the social struggle, of the official representatives of the Church estranges the proletariat from this Church and thus from religion. In the moment that this mistrust is removed--and you all know that the new Christian-socialists, especially in Germany, have taken this as their task,--in the moment when Christianity is presented either as unpartisan in its social influence, as Goehre preaches it, or as directly social-democratic, as Naumann presents it,--in that moment, so far as I see, there will be no reason why the proletariat should maintain an anti-religious character.

In saying this, of course, I assume that religion is adapted to the needs of the proletariat. Whether or not Christianity possesses this adaptability, I do not dare to say. But that it is thus adapted would seem to be indicated by the fact that it became the religion of Rome in its decadence and of the German tribes in the youthful freshness of their civilisation, of feudalism as well as of those stages of civilisation in which the free cities and later the bourgeoisie have had predominance. Then why may it not also be the religion of the proletariat? But it must be presented to the lower classes with all of the joy of life of which Christianity is capable. For the element of asceticism in Christianity pleases little these classes, which press towards air and light and which do not show any inclination to allow the good things of life to be taken from them.

As if overhung with thick clouds of passion, appears now the question as to the attitude of the social movement towards nationality. A great part of the heated discussion on this point, as it seems to me, is due to lack of clearness in thought. It is not so much our German language, as it is our German instinct, that distinguishes between two ideas, rightly but not always sharply separated; we are accustomed to specify them as patriotism and nationalism.

Patriotism, the love of the Fatherland, is indeed a feeling that unconsciously and without effort is held fast in our hearts, and exists therein like love of home and of family. It is an aggregation of impressions, of memories, over which we have no control. It is that indefinable power exercised upon our souls by the sound of the mother tongue, by the harmony of the national song, by many peculiar customs and usages, by the whole history and poetry of the home land. It is that feeling which comes to its fulness only in a strange land, and presses as truly upon the soul of the exiled revolutionist as upon that of the peaceful citizen. I cannot see why this should be the heritage of a particular class. It is a foolish idea that such a feeling may, or can, die out in the great masses of men, so long as there are lands and peoples with their own languages and songs.

Quite different is nationalism--the intelligent presentation, if I may so express it, of national opinion, especially in opposition and enmity to other nations. The modern proletariat does not simply refuse to share this feeling; it actually fights against it.

Here again we meet the same fact that we observed before in connection with the attitude of the proletariat towards religion; they identify the idea of "nationalism" with the ruling classes, and as enemies of the representatives of the idea they turn their hatred against the idea itself. Especially is this so because, in many lands, it is not made easy for the rising working-men's movement to identify itself with the official representatives of the nation;

hate, persecution, repression, are not suitable means to arouse pride in that national structure in which the working men must live together with those from whom all this evil proceeds. At the same time a friendly hand is reached over the national boundary-line by the proletariat of a strange and unfriendly land, by companions in suffering, with similar interests and efforts. Truly it is no wonder that the modern proletariat generally becomes imbued with an anti-national, an international, tendency.

But I hold it to be quite wrong to justify an anti-national theory by this impulsive anti-nationalism. I see in the essence of modern socialism no reason for such an idea. I have explicitly pointed out to you the tendency towards an international understanding and unity on the part of the proletariat. But that is only an artificial abolition of national barriers. Only one who chases after the phantom of a world republic will be able to imagine a social development outside of national limitations. A man will hardly venture to prophesy with certainty, even for only a short time, as to when the social contradictions within a nation shall rival those points of difference at present existing between nations. But it must be clear even to the short-sighted that, so far as we can see, an energetic upholding of national interests can never be entirely unnecessary.

Even if in Western Europe the differences between nations should be so far obviated that only social questions remain in the field, I believe that we could never assume that this Western European civilisation can pursue its course undisturbed and without the admixture of other elements. We must never forget that, as a result of modern means of communication, not only Russian civilisation threatens that of Western Europe, but even the Asiatic more and more strongly presses upon us. The development in Asia which we have seen in the course of the last decade, the rapid advancement of Japan, and now the attempt of China to enter civilisation in order to nibble at the fruits of commerce and to grow out of its narrow circle--this development will doubtless take a course which must of necessity lead to new international complications. I believe that the moment will come when European society as a whole will say to itself: All our mutual differences are of no importance as compared with that which threatens us from this enemy. As an indication of this see the attitude of America towards Asiatic development. There is a case in which the "internationalism" of the proletariat is simply thrown aside; and this would be the case also among the proletariat of Western Europe, if the coolies should begin to swarm over us like rats. An artificial sympathy with the most downtrodden people would prove too weak to restrain a sound national self-interest. So soon as a common enemy threatens the existence of a society it becomes again conscious of its economic interests and rallies to their support; and in the meantime its internal differences are forgotten.

Thus there can be no talk of an essential repudiation of nationalism on the part of the proletariat throughout the world. Discussion of the question concerns only a circle of kindred nations to which one does not want to see the principle of anti-nationalism applied. How such national groups are constituted is a question which it is not necessary for us here to determine, as I desire only to present the essential point in the national problem. You see that, with this discussion, I complete the circle of my thought, and return to that with which I began--the idea that there is, and apparently always will be, an antithesis around which, as around poles, human history circles, the social and the national. That is something which the proletariat should never forget.

CHAPTER VIII

LESSONS

"+Polemos pater panton.+"

War is the father of all things.

Can we draw lessons from this historical review of the social movement? I think we can, on many points; to show you what these lessons are will be my effort in this last lecture. Perhaps I may exert some influence upon the judgment of those who personally stand outside of the present social strife and desire to be merely passionless observers. And I shall be glad if, here and there among those actively engaged in the struggle, some shall be found who will recognise the justice of what I may say.

It seems to me that the first impression to be made upon anyone by quiet observation of the social movement must be that it is necessary and unavoidable. As a mountain torrent, after a thunder-storm, must dash down into the valley according to "iron, unchangeable law," so must the stream of social agitation pour itself onward. This is the first thing for us to understand, that something of great and historic importance is developing before our eyes; to recognise "that in all that happens and is accomplished in connection with this movement we are in the midst of a great process of world history which with elementary force takes hold of individuals and even nations, and concerning which it is as wrong short-sightedly to deny the fact as inadequately to struggle against it." (Lorenz von Stein.) Probably there are some who believe that the social movement is merely the malicious work of a few agitators, or that the social democracy has been "brought up by Bismarck," and the like; probably there are some who naturally are forced to the false idea that some medicine or charm can drive away this fatal poison out of the social body. What a delusion! What a lack of intelligence and insight as to the nature of all social history! If anything has resulted from my investigation I hope it is this--a recognition of the historic necessity of the social movement.

But we must advance to a further admission--that the modern social movement, at least in its main features, exists necessarily as it is. Among these main features I include the object that it sets before itself, the socialistic ideal; also the means which it chooses for the accomplishment of this ideal,--class strife. I have already attempted to show you why these points must be allowed as the necessary result of existing conditions.

Now shall we who do not stand in the ranks of those who struggle for the new social order, shall we who only tremble for the permanence of that which seems to us necessary for the upholding of our civilisation--shall we be greatly pained and troubled at the present condition of things as thus shown?

I think it hardly necessary to excite ourselves over the "dangers" of any socialistic order of society in the future. We who know that all social order is only the expression of specific economic relations can face what comes with indifference; so long as these arrangements of economic life are not given up, especially so long as the character of the persons involved, is not completely changed, no power on earth, no party--be it ever so revolutionary--can succeed in establishing a new social order for humanity. And if these conditions are at any time fulfilled--then will be the time to look further.

But it is not this socialistic ideal of the future that principally causes anxiety to so many men. It is rather the form in which this ideal is striven for; it is that word of terror, uttered by Philistines both male and female--class strife.

I must acknowledge that for me this idea has in it nothing at all terrible, rather the opposite. Is it really true that, even if strife rules throughout society, man must give up entirely the hope of a further and successful development of humanity? Is it really true that all culture, all the noblest acquirements of the race, are endangered by that strife?

First let me dispel the delusion that "class strife" is identical with civil war, with petroleum, dynamite, the stiletto, and the barricades. The forms of class strife are many. Every trade union, every social-democratic election, every strike, is a manifestation of this strife. And it seems to me that such internal struggle, such conflict of different interests and ideas, is not only without danger to our civilisation, but on the contrary will be the source of much that is desirable. I think that the old proverb is true as applied even to social strife, "+Polemos pater panton.+" It is only through struggle that the most beautiful flowers of human existence bloom. It is only struggle that raises the great masses of the common people to a higher level of humanity. Whatever of culture is now forced upon the masses comes to them through struggle; the only warrant for the hope that they can be developed into new and higher forms of culture lies in the fact that they must rise through their efforts, that step by step they must fight for their rights. It is struggle alone that builds character and arouses enthusiasm, for nations as for classes. Let me remind you of a beautiful saying of Kant's, that expresses the same thought: "Thanks to nature for intolerance, for envious and emulous self-seeking, for the insatiable desire to have and to rule! Without this, all the desirable qualities of humanity would lie eternally undeveloped. Man wants peace, but Nature knows better what is necessary for him; she wants strife."

And why lose courage, as we see that even in social life struggle is the solution? To me this seems no reason for despair. I rejoice in this law of the history of the world; that is a happy view of life which makes struggle as the central point of existence.

But we should never forget that as conflict is the developer of what is good, so it may also be the disturber and destroyer of all civilisation. It does not lead only and by necessity to a higher life, it is not necessarily the beginning of a new culture: it can also betoken the end of the old, and of all, human existence.

For this reason I think that we should never lose sight of two great ideas in this strife.

First, all social struggle should be determinedly within legal bounds. Thus only can the sanctity of the idea of right remain uninjured. Without this we plunge into chaos. Man must struggle in the name of right against that which he considers wrong, upon the basis of existing right. Man must respect this right because it has become right, and passes for such; and he must not forget that our fathers struggled not less intensely for that right which to-day we hold, and have had in heart not less enthusiasm than their sons for the right of the future. Only thus can a man awaken and sustain faith in that which at some future time shall be right.

This exhortation addresses itself in like manner to both parties in the struggle; to those who are now in power, not less than to those who are carrying on the social agitation. Intra muros peccatur et extra! There is sin within, as without, the walls.

The same is true of a second demand, which must be developed in the name of culture and humanity within these struggling parties, if the social strife is not to be a war of extermination. It must be carried on with proper weapons, not with poisoned arrows. How greatly have both sides been to blame in this respect! How difficult it is to keep out of the battle on the one side bitterness, mendacity, malice; on the other side brutality, derision, violence! How readily does the one opponent charge dishonour or bad motive against the other! How repellent, how offensive, too often, is the tone in which opinion is expressed! Must that be? Is that necessary for energetic assertion of one's standpoint? Does a man think that he loses anything by conceding that his opponent is an honourable man and by assuming that truth and honour will control in the dealings of his adversary? I do not think so. The man who places himself really in the struggle, who sees that in all historic strife is the germ of whatever occurs, should be able easily to conduct this strife in a noble way, to respect his opponent as a man, and to attribute to him motives no less pure than his own.

Then is not the social struggle, according to this idea of it, as necessary as a thunder-storm in a heavy atmosphere? He who sees in the struggle something artificial, produced by bad men, may perhaps attribute to the creator of the disturbance bad motives for this knavery, for this frivolous and malicious upsetting of social rest. But he who understands that the struggle arises necessarily out of the constitution of social life, and that it is only a warfare between two great principles, each of which has been, and must be, constituted by a combination of objective circumstances--he who looks at differences of idea as to the world and life which arise from the fact of different standpoints and which are the necessary occasion of differences in conditions of life--this one will come to the conviction that even his opponent stands on much the same grounds as he himself; that not personal baseness, but the compelling force of fate, has placed him in a position such that he must be an opponent. Then will it be easy, I think, to respect the other man, to refrain from suspicion and contempt, to battle with him openly and honourably. Shall we extol the Geneva Convention, which humanised warfare, as a fruit of advanced culture; and yet within our kingdom, like barbarians, without any consideration for the opponent, fly one upon another with dishonourable weapons?

In this the development of English social agitation can serve as a model. It points out to us how men may conduct in social life a moral and civilised warfare. Even upon the Continent, I hope, will the more humane form of struggle reach acceptance, if only because it springs of necessity from a deeper conception of what class strife really is. So long as the battle rages legally and honourably, we need not worry about the future of our civilisation.

Schiller's lines show how undisturbed we may be at the social struggle:

"A full life is what I want, And swinging and swaying, to and fro, Upon the rising and falling waves of fortune. For a man becomes stunted in quietness of life; Idleness and rest are the grave of energy.

* * * * *

But war develops strength. It raises all to a level above what is ordinary, It even gives courage to the cowardly."

CHRONICLE OF THE SOCIAL MOVEMENT (1750-1896).

These tables contain the first attempt to make a synchronistic presentation of the most important dates in the modern social, that is, the proletarian, movement. We here specify these dates for the chief countries, England, France, Germany; and as well for the international activity of the working-men's movement. In addition, the most important occurrences in the development of capitalism and of social legislation, so far as they have relation of cause or effect with the social movement, are indicated in heavy type.

YEAR	ENGLAND	FRANCE	GERMANY	INTERNATIONAL
1750-1800	Notable inventions of modern machinery: (1764-75. Spinning machine. 1785-90. The machine loom. 1799. Paper machine.) Rapid development of the great centres of industry. "Machine Riots." Petitions to forbid legally machines and to reintroduce the Elizabethan trade ordinances. Laws for the protection of machines.		1780. The puddling process. 1790. Steam engine. manufactories, ordinances.	
1776	Adam Smith (1723-90). "Wealth of Nations."			
1796		Babeuf's conspiracy, or "The Equals."		
1800	Robert Owen (1771-1858; chief writings: "A New View of Society," "Book of the New Moral World"). Enters the Dale manufactory at Lanark. Rigorous prohibition of combination.			
1808		Charles Fourier's (1772-1837) first great book appears: "Theorie de quatre mouvements" (1822: "Theorie de l'unite universelle," 1824: "Le nouveau monde industriel et societaire").		
1813-1814	Complete removal of the Elizabethan trade restrictions.			
1815-1832	Struggle of the proletariat for political rights.			
1819	The "Savannah" arrives at Liverpool.			
1821		Saint Simon's (1760-1825) chief work, "Du Systeme Industriel," appears (1825: "Nouveau Christianisme").		
1825	More liberal coalition law. Rise of the Trade Unions.			
1830	Opening of the Manchester-Liverpool Railroad.			
1830-1848		July Kingdom. Rapid economic development; "Enrichissez-vous, messieurs."		
1830-1832		The movement of Bazard and Enfantin, the disciples of Saint Simon.		
1831		Insurrection of the silk workers in Lyons: "Vivre en travaillant ou mourir en combattant."		
1833				

|Beginnings of | | | |specific | | | |legislation for | | | |working-men. | | | |
| | | 1834 |Grand national | |Founding of the | |consolidated | |German |
|trade union, in | |Zollverein. | |the spirit of | |Beginnings of | |Robert
Owen. | |national | | | |industry. | | | | | 1836 | |Beginning of the | |The
"Junger | |"Journalistic" | |Deutschland" in | |period of | |Switzerland. |
|Fourierism under | |"Bund der | |Victor | |Gerechten"; | |Considerant. |
|with its | |Appearance of the| |central office | |Christian | |in London after
| |socialists (De La| |1840. | |Mennais); the | | | |"Icarian | | |
|Communism" of | | | |Cabet (Voyage en | | | |Icarie, 1840). | | | | | | 1836
| |Beginning of the | | | |economic unions | | | |(Buchez, born | | | |1796).
| | | | | | 1837-|The Chartist | | | 1848 |movement. Six | | | |points. Lovett.
| | | |Feargus O'Connor.| | | | | | 1839-|Activity of | | | 1854 |Thomas
Carlyle | | | |("Past and | | | |Present," 1843), | | | |and the Christian| | |
socialists				(Charles				Kingsley, Thomas				Hughes, J.D.		
Maurice).							1839	|Louis Blanc			|(1813-1882):		
"Organisation du				travail."						1840	Rowland Hill's	Fullest	
penny postage is	development of			introduced. The	anarchistic-	
telegraph is	communistic			first applied to	clubbism and			English
conspiracy in			railroads.	"Societe des				Travailleurs		
egalitaires."							P.J. Proudhon				(1809-1865).				"Qu'est-ce
que la				propriete?"						1844	The Pioneers of		Loom riots in
Rochdale.		Langenbielau u.				Peterswaldau;				tumults of		
working-men in				Breslau,				Warmbrunn, and				other places.
			1847			|The "Bund der			|Gerechten"			|changes itself		
into the "Bund			|der			|Kommunisten"			|and takes as			|its
platform			|the			|"Communistic			|Manifesto,"			|written by
Karl			|Marx (1818-			|1883) and			|Frederick			|Engels		
(1820-1895).				"Proletarians				of all lands,				unite		
yourselves."				1848		The Paris	Communistic			"February
agitation on the			Revolution."	Rhine, started by			Karl Marx and	
Proletarian	associates.			representatives	("Neue Rheinische		in the
Zeitung," 1. VI.			provisional	48-19. V. 49).			government;	The
German			Louis Blanc and	working-men's			Albert. 23. u.	movement
captured			24. VI., "June	by the			insurrection."	hand-workers.	

|The proletariat |Stefan Born. W. | | |defeated in |Weitling. | | |street fights. | | | | | | 1850-|England's | | | 1880 |position of | | | |industrial | | | |monopoly in the | | | |markets of the | | | |world. Rapid | | | |development of | | | |the trade unions.| | | | | | | 1850-| | |Stern regulations| 1856 | | |of the various | | | |German | | | |governments and | | | |of the | | | |Confederation for| | | |the complete | | | |repression of the| | | |working-men's | | | |movement. | | | | | | | |Gradual founding | | | |of working-men's | | | |associations and | | | |"culture unions" | | | |(Schulze- | | | |Delitzsch). | | | | | 1851-| |Severe laws of | | 1854 | |Napoleon III. for| | | |the repression of| | | |all social | | | |agitation. | | | | | | 1851 |Founding of the | | |First World's |United Society of| | |Exposition in |Machinists. | | |London. | | | | 1852 | | | |The "League of | | | |Communists" | | | |dissolves. | | | | 1862 | | |Deputation of | | | |working-men from | | | |Leipzig to the | | | |leaders of the | | | |national union in| | | |Berlin; "Honorary| | | |members!" | | | | | 1863 | | |Ferdinand | | | |Lassalle | | | |(1825-1864; 1858,| | | |"Heraklit, der | | | |Dunkle"; 1861, | | | |"System der | | | |erworbenen | | | |Rechte"); 1. | | | |III.: "Offenes | | | |Antwortschreiben | | | |an das Central | | | |Kommittee zur | | | |Berufung eines | | | |allgemeinen | | | |deutscher | | | |Arbeiter- | | | |Kongresses | | | |zu Leipzig." | | | | | | | |23. V.: Founding | | | |of the general | | | |German | | | |working-men's | | | |movement by | | | |Lassalle. | | | |Disruption after | | | |Lassalle's death | | | |in the male line | | | |(Becker, J.B. von| | | |Schweitzer) and | | | |in the female | | | |line (Countess | | | |Hatzfeld). | | | | | 1864 | | | |Founding of the | | | |International | | | |Working-Men's | | | |Association by | | | |the delegates | | | |of different | | | |nations at the | | | |World's | | | |Exposition in | | | |London. | | | |Inaugural | | | |address and a | | | |constitution by | | | |Karl Marx. He | | | |remains the | | | |veiled leader | | | |of the | | | |"International." | | | |The general | | | |office of the | | | |Society is in | | | |London. | | | | 1865 | | |Beginnings of | | | |trade agitation; | | | |the tobacco | | | |workers; (1866 | | | |the printers). | | | | | 1867 | | |Bismarck forces |Appearance of | | |the general, |the first | | |equal, secret, |volume of | | |and direct |"Capital" by | | |ballot. |Karl Marx. | | | | 1868 | | | |Founding of the | | | |"Alliance | | | |international | | | |de la | | |

|democratic | | | |sociale" by | | | |Michael Bakunin | | | |(1814-1876), | | | |with | | | |anarchistic | | | |tendencies in | | | |clear | | | |opposition to | | | |the Marxist | | | |ideas. | | | | 1869 | | |Liberal trade | | | |regulation for | | | |the German | | | |Empire. Rapid | | | |development of | | | |capitalism, | | | |especially after | | | |the war. | | | | | | |The founding of | | | |the "Social- | | | |Democratic | | | |Working-men's | | | |Party" at the | | | |Congress at | | | |Eisenach: the | | | |so-called | | | |"Ehrlichen." | | | |August Bebel | | | |(born 1840); | | | |Wilhelm | | | |Liebknecht (born | | | |1826). Founding | | | |of the | | | |"Hirsch-Duncker" | | | |trade unions. | | | | | | |The General | | | |Assembly of the | | | |German Catholic | | | |unions decides | | | |upon | | | |participation in | | | |the social | | | |movement from the| | | |Catholic | | | |standpoint. | | | | | 1871 |Trade-union act, |The Paris | | |supplemented in |Commune. | | |1875, sanctions | | | |the trade-union | | | |agitation. | | | | | | 1872 | | | |Congress of the | | | |"I.A.A." at | | | |Hague. | | | |Exclusion of | | | |Bakunin and his | | | |faction, who | | | |yet for a time | | | |find a | | | |standing-place | | | |in the | | | |"Federation | | | |juraissienne." | | | |Removal of the | | | |general office | | | |of the "I.A.A." | | | |to New York. | | | | 1875 | | |Fusion of the | | | |followers of | | | |Lassalle with the| | | |Eisenachers at | | | |the congress in | | | |Gotha. The | | | |"compromise | | | |platform" of | | | |Gotha. | | | |Gotha. | | | | | 1876 | |First general | |The "I.A.A." | |French | |formally | |Working-Men's | | dissolves. | |Congress at | | | |Paris. | | | | | | 1877 | | | |The Ghent | | | |"World's | | | |Congress." | | | |Attempt for the | | | |reconciliation | | | |of the | | | |Bakunists and | | | |the Marxists | | | |miscarries. A | | | |general union | | | |of | | | |"International | | | |Socialism" is | | | |resolved upon | | | |by the | | | |Marxists, but | | | |does not come | | | |to importance. | | | | 1879-| | | | 1890 | | |Law concerning | | | |the socialists. | | | | | | |Destruction of | | | |working-men's | | | |organizations. | | | |Removal of the | | | |strength of the | | | |agitation to | | | |other lands. | | | |("Social- | | | |demokrat" in | | | |Zurich and | | | |London.) | | | | | 1878 | | |Founding of a | | | |conservative | | | |Christian | | | |Socialism by | | | |Stoecker. | | | | | 1879 | |Working-Men's | | | |Congress in | | | |Marseilles for | | | |the first time | | | |gives power to | | | |the | | | |Collectivists. | | | | | | 1880 |

Working-Men's Congress in Havre; rupture between the moderates and the radicals. The latter constitute themselves as a "Parti ouvrier revolutionnaire socialiste francais."

1881 Founding of the Social-Democratic Federation under the control of Marxian influence.

1882 Working-Men's Congress at St. Etienne. Division between the Possibilists and the "Guesdists." The former split, at a later time, into "Bronssists" ("Federation des travailleurs socialiste de France"), Marxists, and "Allemanists" (Parti ouvrier socialiste revolutionnaire francais).

1883 Founding of the Beginning of Fabian Society. governmental working-man's assurance; Insurance for the sick; 1884 Insurance against accident; 1890, Insurance for the sick and aged.

1884 A new "Syndicate" law favors the development of the trade-union movement.

1885 Founding of the "Societe d'economie sociale" by Benoit Malon, the center of the "independent" socialists ("Parti socialiste independant").

1886 Founding of the "Federation des syndicate" at the Congress at Lyons.

1887 Beginning of the "new Unionism;" the trade-union movement reaches lower strata of the working men with socialistic tendencies (John Burns, Tom Mann, Keir Hardie). Independent labor party.

1889 Two International Congresses of Working-men at Paris constituted by the "Possibilists" and the "Guesdists," proclaim as the salvation of the proletariat in general the legal enactment of an eight-hour day of work, and the celebration of May 1st as the working-men's holiday. (The first International Association Congress under the new enumeration.)

1890 The Trade-Union Congress in Liverpool endorses a legal establishment of the eight-hour work-day by a The first May festival of the proletariat in all civilized lands. the eight-hour work-day by a The first |vote of 193 to | | |International |155. | | |Miners' | | | |Congress at | | | |Jolimont. | | | | 1890 | | | |International | | | |Working-Men's | | | |Protection | | | |Conference in | | | |Berlin called | | | |by Kaiser | | | |Wilhelm II., | | | |attended by | | | |delegates from | | | |13 nations. | | | | 1891 | | |A new party |Second | | |programme for the|International | | |Social-Democracy |Working-Men's | | |founded |Congress at | | |definitely upon |Brussels. | | |Marxian | | | |principles: the |Exclusion of | | |so-called "Erfurt|the Anarchists. | | |programme." | | | | |Encyclical of | | |Separation of the|Leo XIII., | | |"independent" |"Rerum | | |socialists of |novarum," | | |anarchistic |defines the | | |tendency from the|programme of | | |Social-Democracy.|all | | | |Catholic-social | | |agitation. | | | | 1892 | |Congress of |First general | | |socialists at |trade-union | | |Marseilles |Congress at | | |resolves upon an |Halberstadt. | | |agrarian | | | |programme with | | |recognition of | | | |small peasantry | | | |holdings. | | | | | | 1893 | |First Congress of|The Social- |Third | |the "Federation |Democracy comes |International | |de Bourses du |out of the |Working-Men's | |Travail." |parliamentary |Congress in | | |elections as the |Zurich; the | | |strongest party |English | | |in Germany--with |trade-unions | | |1,786,738 votes. |deliberate | | |officially in | | | |union with the | | | |continental | | | |socialists. | | | | 1894 |The Trade-Union | |Beginning of a |First |Congress at |Democratic- |International |Norwich declares | |Christian-Social |Weaver's |itself by a | |agitation by |Congress at |majority vote for|Pastor Naumann |Manchester. |a communization | |(Die Hilfe). |of the means of | | |production. | | | | | | | 1896 | | | |Fourth | | |International | | | |Working-Men's | | | |Congress in | | | |London. ------+---

--------------+------------------+------------------+------------------